**When life is pulling you in all directions...
when problems overshadow your dreams...
turn to these books for guidance and
affirmation:**

Stressed-Out But Hangin' Tough by **Andrea Stephens**
An easy-to-read guide to help overcome the pressures that
can sometimes overwhelm you. Andrea Stephens counsels
you on handling major sources of stress, including school,
dating, money matters, self-image, and more. Now you
can beat stress before it burns you out!

Tough Turf by **Bill Sanders**
In these pages, Bill Sanders reveals the secret to believing
in yourself. You can be assured that no matter where you
come from...what you look like...or how popular you are
...you've got what it takes to be a winner!

Great books for building your relationship with God:

Goalposts: Devotions for Girls by **Bill Sanders**
Hot Trax: Devotions for Girls by **Ken Abraham**
Outtakes: Devotions for Girls by **Bill Sanders**
Graffiti: Devotions for Girls by **J. David Schmidt**

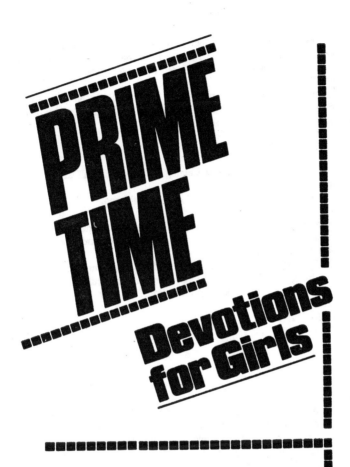

PRIME TIME

Devotions for Girls

Andrea Stephens

Fleming H. Revell
A Division of Baker Book House
Grand Rapids, Michigan 49506

Scripture verses marked TLB are taken from The Living Bible, Copyright © 1971 by Tyndale House Publishers, Wheaton, Ill. Used by permission.

Scripture quotations marked NAS are from the New American Standard Bible, © The Lockman Foundation 1960, 1962, 1963, 1968, 1971, 1972, 1973, 1975, 1977.

Scripture texts identified NIV are from the Holy Bible, New International Version, copyright © 1973, 1978, 1984 International Bible Society. Used by permission of Zondervan Bible Publishers.

Library of Congress Cataloging-in-Publication Data

Stephens, Andrea.
    Prime time devotions for girls / Andrea Stephens.
        p.   cm.
    Summary: A collection of devotional readings for girls, covering
such areas as self-image, prayer, temptation, stress, and direction in life.
    ISBN 0-8007-5390-9
    1. Teenage girls—Prayer-books and devotions—English.   2. Teenage
girls—Religious life.   3. Devotional calendars—Juvenile
literature.   [1. Prayer books and devotions.   2. Christian life.]
I. Title.
BV4860.S74   1991
242'. 633—dc20
                                                    90-22459
                                                      CIP
                                                       AC

Copyright © 1991 by Andrea Stephens
Published by Fleming H. Revell
a division of Baker Book House Company
P.O. Box 6287, Grand Rapids, MI 49516-6287

ISBN: 0-8007-5390-9

Fourth printing, December 1992

Printed in the United States of America

To
my
teeter-
totter
girls
who
struggle
with
their
faith.
Here's
the
stuff
you
need
to
know.
Use
it
wisely!

Love,
Andrea

A heartfelt thanks to:

My guest authors and special friends, Barbra, Karen, Lenne Jo, Carolyn, Judy, and Nell. I appreciate your willingness to share your guidance with these young ladies!

My youth group girls at Covington Presbyterian Church who read parts of this manuscript, as well as Barbra, Francie, Bill, and Carol.

My friend Carol Mulker who once again joyfully typed this manuscript, taking a heavy load off my shoulders!

And to my caring family and friends for their much needed prayer support!

Contents

A Word From the Author   13

1 **Chill Out!**   19
   Anger

2 **Remember Who You Are**   25
   Reputation

3 **All Clogged Up!**   31
   Communication

4 **Anchors Aweigh!**   37
   God's Stability

5 **The Right Combination**   43
   Salvation

6 **The Invisible Friend**   49
   The Holy Spirit

7 **Beauty—It's More Than Skin-Deep!** 55
Inner Beauty

8 **Best Friends** 61
Friendship

9 **Total Fitness** 67
Body and Spirit Nutrition

10 **Hope in the Night** 73
Assurance

11 **I've Got PMS!** 79
A Joyful Heart

12 **Oh No! It's Sunday Again** 85
Church

13 **There's Always a Way Out** 91
Temptation

14 **Hospitality Plus!** 97
Hospitality

15 **A Spoke in the Wheel of Life** 103
Team Effort for God

16 **Stop Checking Up on Me!** 109
Gaining Trust

17 **The Little Brick Schoolhouse** 115
School

18 **Waiting on Dreams** 121
Waiting on the Lord

19 Me? A Missionary?   127
     Teen Missions

20 Sunglasses and Sex   133
     God's Protective Laws

21 What a Mess I Am!   139
     Getting Organized

22 New Attitude   145
     Attitudes

23 The Visitation   151
     Comforting Others

24 He's So Fine   157
     Dating

25 Working Girl   163
     Work

26 Playful Pups   169
     A Parent's Role

     About the Guest Authors   175

A Word From the Author

Read This Before You Begin!

Piles of homework, student council meetings, cheerleading practice, boys, piano lessons, swim meets, youth group, boys, tennis tournaments, drama club rehearsal, band practice, your new job, television, and boys! There are so many things pulling you in different directions, competing for your time. And there are only twenty-four hours in each day! Girls are busy, busy, busy!

Plus, in this teenage time of life when you are struggling to figure out who you are, it seems everyone has an opinion about everything! Your parents say one thing, your friends say another, your social life is pulling you in one direction, your church in another, some of the music you listen to says to forget God and just please yourself. So many voices! Who are you supposed to listen to? Who can you believe?

That's why more than ever before, you need to set aside some Prime Time with God! Spending time learning from God's Word and having heart-to-heart prayer time with Jesus will give you the guidance, wisdom, and strength you need to make it in the nineties. So, I wrote this book to help you. I've included the important stuff you need to know.

Here's How to Use It

Pick a time five or six days each week when you are awake and alert to do a short study. I suggest trying to study at the same time each day—before school, after dinner. Don't do it late at night on your bed when you're ready to fall asleep. Chances are you won't remember a thing the next day!

Each week you will study one topic. Begin each day with prayer, asking God to open your heart and mind to His truth. Now, dig in! Look up the Scriptures. Write your responses. Ask yourself how you can start living out what you're learning. Then, close each day with the suggested prayer, including other needs you want to tell God about. Listen intently for God's answers. Watch closely for His hand working in your life.

At the end of the week, review the Scriptures you read each day and pick out your favorite one. Now write it out in the space provided. Challenge yourself to memorize it. Hide it away in your heart. You can do it!

If you start to fall behind in your study, don't quit!

Just pick up where you left off or start fresh with a new week. Just do your best and be flexible.

You may find it helpful to share this devotional book with a sister or a girl friend. It can be used for individual or small group study. I recommend that you use a New American Standard or Living Bible to accompany this book.

I pray these devotionals will change your life. It wasn't until I started studying God's Word for myself that I was able to really get my life on the right path. My life took on a whole new meaning. I hope these studies will do the same for you. Enjoy your Prime Time with the Lord!

Your friend,

Andrea Stephens

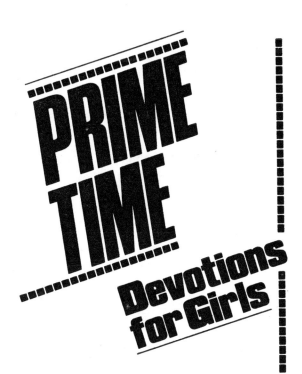

Chill Out!

If you are angry, don't sin by nursing your grudge.
Don't let the sun go down with you still angry—get
over it quickly.

Ephesians 4:26 TLB

■■■■■■■■■■■■■■■■■■■■■■■■■■■■■■■■

"I'm so ticked off," Karen hissed out as she ran the
dreadful scene through her mind again. "How could
Mark be such a jerk? How could he have the nerve to
embarrass me like that? I'll get back at him. I'll make
him pay. I'll—"

WAIT A MINUTE, KAREN, her conscience yelled
back.

The discussion they had had last week in Sunday
school suddenly struck her mind like lightning. She
could hear her teacher's words echoing in her mind:

> "It's okay to be angry about certain things, but don't
> let that anger make you sin. And never go to sleep
> angry or still in a fight with someone. Get rid of anger
> quickly before you give Satan a chance to lead you
> into doing the wrong thing."

The message rang loud and clear, racing through Karen's mind. Was she wrong to be mad at Mark? He had hurt her and belittled her in front of her friends.

There are situations in life that will cause you to be angry. Anger itself is not wrong. It's often an involuntary emotion that needs to be controlled. But beware, there is good anger and bad anger. Being angry at poverty, homelessness, abortion, social injustice, mistreatment of minorities, or evil is valid and it is okay to be mad at these things. This kind of anger can motivate us to take action against these situations. It is constructive anger. But bad anger, which includes most anger, tends to be negative. Jealousy over a friend's good fortune, being criticized unfairly, being stuck in a slow moving line, getting beat in a game, someone's lying to you, and hurt feelings cause the kind of anger that needs to be dealt with quickly because it leads to sin.

Let the Lord help you chill out and get rid of your negative anger. Pray, surrender it to Him, telling Him all about what happened and how you feel. Now, open your heart and allow Him to give you the desire and ability to forgive and forget the situation that caused the anger in the first place. Karen finally did, and now she and Mark are friends again.

Lord, I find it very easy to get mad at my friends, parents, and brothers and sisters. Letting go of the anger is the hard part. I need Your help on this. Thanks. Amen.

Prime Time This Week

Just as there is good and bad anger, there are good and bad ways to handle your anger. We have already learned that if we feed our grudge when we're angry and refuse to get over our anger quickly, it can cause us to do something we will regret. This week you'll look at ways to deal and not deal with your anger. And you'll find out more of what the Bible has to say about anger. Pray each day that these lessons will help you chill out when your anger gets hot and heavy!

Monday

Repressing your angry feelings means to ignore them, not admit they are there! Repressing your anger keeps it in your subconscious where it can lead to depression. What could be some results of handling your anger like this? Read Genesis 4:5–8. What did repressed anger do to Cain? It made him even more mad and led him to killing his own brother, Abel

Prime Prayer: Ask the Lord to make you aware of your anger so you can heal it, not hide it.

Tuesday

Suppressing your anger means holding it in. It's like stuffing or swallowing your anger. But, you still know it's there! Suppressed **anger** shows up in the body through headaches, stomach troubles, skin disorders. Suppressing may lead to overeating, rebellion, alcohol abuse, or running away from your troubles any way you can. If a person takes her anger out on herself like this, what could the results be? *The results could be dangerous or even fatal. She should talk about her anger*

Prime Prayer: Ask God to show you if you have any of these symptoms because of anger. If so, ask Him to help you solve the situation.

Wednesday

Revenge! Anger that leads to negative action is dangerous. Anger causes pent-up energy if it's not nipped in the bud. Revenge can result. Read Romans 12:19. Is it your place to get back at someone? How can you leave the situation in God's hands? *Leave your enemy to god and pray to him to take your troubles away & show you how to deal with it.*

Prime Prayer: Pray for self-control and the ability to forgive the person you are angry at. Let God handle it!

Thursday

Expressing your anger. Scripture has a lot to say about this. See Ephesians 4:15. Why is speaking the truth in love more effective than screaming, blaming, and hating? Now read James 1:19. How would being slow to anger help in your relationships and in controlling your anger? _____

_____

_____

_____

Prime Prayer: Ask the Lord to help you speak lovingly to the person you are angry at so you can finally clear the air with him. Also pray to be *slow* to get angry.

Friday

Do you associate with people who have quick tempers and frequent outbursts? Do you have them? Beware. Check out Proverbs 19:19 and Proverbs 22:24, 25. Why do angry people continually need to be rescued? What may happen to you if you hang out with hotheaded people? _____

_____

_____

_____

Prime Prayer: Ask the Lord to make you an even-tempered person so you will be a good example to others.

THIS WEEK'S MEMORY VERSE: PICK IT! WRITE IT! REMEMBER IT!

_____

_____

_____

_____

_____

Remember Who
You Are

If you must choose, take a good name rather than
great riches; for to be held in loving esteem is better
than silver and gold.

Proverbs 22:1 TLB

■■■■■■■■■■■■■■■■■■■■■■■■■■■■■■■■■■

July 19, 1990, was a sad day for baseball hero Pete
Rose. He was sentenced to five months in prison,
three months in a halfway house, one thousand hours
of community service, and was blasted with a $50,000
fine. Why? After an incredible baseball career setting
the all-time record of 4,256 hits, a budding career as
manager of the Cincinnati Reds, and being up for
nomination into the Baseball Hall of Fame, legendary
Pete Rose took a nosedive, because of his gambling
habit and tax evasion.

USA Today records Pete Rose as saying at his trial, "I
lost my dignity, I lost my self-respect." But most harmful, through it all, Pete Rose lost his reputation and
smeared his own name. During his career, Rose made a

lot of money, but now it meant nothing. He had lost his name.

To have a "good name" means to have a good reputation. Your reputation is based on your character: who you are, what you do, who you hang out with, and what kinds of things you do or don't do.

My husband's mom, Nell, knew how valuable a good and honorable reputation would be to her kids when they were teens. When Bill was headed out the door for his big football game or softball tournament, an important date, or just a night out with the guys, his mom would say, "Now, Bill, remember who you are and who you belong to." Nell wasn't trying to lay a guilt trip on her son; she was simply reminding him that he was her son and belonged to a family that was good, hardworking, and well respected in the community. More important, she was reminding Bill that he was first and foremost a Christian, that he belonged to his Heavenly Father, and that he needed to be representing God by controlling his conduct, plus selecting the right friends and activities.

The same lesson applies to all Christians. If you get mixed up in the wrong crowd or activities, you'll ruin your reputation, shaming your own name. A good reputation is a hard thing to earn back once it is tainted.

Teen years are a time to test your wings and find out what life is all about. But beware. Be selective. Be wise. Be mindful of the fact you are representing your Lord.

Dear Father God, the name Christian means follower of Christ. Remind me when I am tempted or am doing less than my best, that I am representing You. I truly want to bring glory and honor to Your name. Amen.

Prime Time This Week

This week think about your own reputation. What beliefs or activities have contributed to the reputation you have gained? Some teens forget they represent their parents, themselves, and their Lord the minute they walk out the front door. Yet, others realize that because they choose to represent Christ they may have to put up with some put-downs! Let's see what the Bible has to say.

Monday

Colossians 3:17 reminds you that in all you do, you represent your Lord. How can this guide you in making decisions about your life-style? _____

_____

_____

_____

Prime Prayer: Ask Jesus to make you a good representative for Him in all you do and say.

Tuesday

As Pete Rose found out and Proverbs 22:1 states, a good reputation is better than money. In fact, money can't buy a favorable reputation. Money comes and goes. A good reputation is lasting. What type of things will earn a person a good reputation? _____

_____

_____

_____

Prime Prayer: Ask the Lord to help you to start today to do the things that will earn you a favorable reputation.

Wednesday

All Christians at some time face ridicule for following Christ. It's not easy being made fun of, but don't be ashamed. Suffering for Jesus brings glory to God and respect to you in the eyes of other Christians. Check it out! Write down what the Bible teaches in Philippians 2:29, 30; 1 Peter 4:13–16; and Acts 5:41, 42. _____

_____

_____

_____

Prime Prayer: Ask God to help you endure suffering for His sake, knowing that your being obedient to Him makes Him happy.

Thursday

Read the story in Acts 5:34–40. Was Gamaliel a respected person? Did the crowd listen to his opinion? Why are respected people put in leadership positions? Why do others honor their opinions? _____

_____

_____

_____

Prime Prayer: Pray to be the kind of person others can respect and trust.

Friday

How do you get a reputation? By your attitudes and actions. It's your choice as to the kind of teen others see you as. Make this your goal: To be held in loving esteem by others and to keep your name good (Proverbs 22:1). Name two key attitudes you could change or activities you could join that would make your reputation better. _____

_____

_____

_____

Prime Prayer: If you need a new reputation, ask the Lord to show you how you need to change so others will slowly begin to think differently of you.

■■■■■■■■■■■■■■■■■■■■■■■■■■■■■■■■■■■■■

THIS WEEK'S MEMORY VERSE: PICK IT! WRITE IT! REMEMBER IT!

_____

_____

_____

_____

_____

■■■■■■■■■■■■■■■■■■■■■■■■■■■■■■■■■■■■■

All Clogged Up!

Bearing with one another, and forgiving each other,
whoever has a complaint against anyone; just as the
Lord forgave you, so also should you.

Colossians 3:13 NAS

■ ■

What happens to the kitchen sink when Mom pours
hot cooking oil down the drain, then Dad eats practically
a whole cantaloupe and stuffs that rind down there, then
little brother scrapes mud off his boots in there, and then
you come along to rinse off your hands? Clogged! That
poor sink gets backed up and clogged. The same thing
happens in the tub when too much tangled hair tries to
make its way to the bottom of the pipes!

Clogging occurs when too many undissolved things or
too much garbage gets all jammed up, keeping anything
else from passing through. It's like choking the pipe.

A clog can form in other things besides pipes. Clogs
can develop between people, too. They stop up our
communication—we can't seem to talk freely and easily.
Our relationship seems choked.

Does this ever happen between you and your parents? Ever want to talk to your mom or dad but words don't come? Or maybe you get the feeling they're upset, busy, tired, or they don't understand your feelings. Communication clog!

Colossians 3:13 gives some great advice on how to get that clog cleared up! First, it says to bear with each other. What do you think *bear* means? To bear with someone means to help support them, help hold them up in prayer, and be there for them through tough times. It's more than just tolerating them until they get rid of their problem. Perhaps your parents are in a situation that is troubling them. Maybe it's their jobs or the family finances. See what you can do to take the pressure off and help them through it. Pitch in with the laundry, make dinner, cut the lawn without being asked or paid! When your parents have their own problems off their minds, they'll be more focused on talking with you and, in turn, helping you bear your troubles. Galatians 6:2 tells us to bear *one another's* burdens!

Second, we are to forgive each other because unforgiveness and holding grudges are major communication cloggers! Whether you offended them or they offended you, be the one to go to your parents and ask for forgiveness. Likewise, you must forgive them. After all, the Lord has forgiven us, and we know how good that feels. There are no strings attached. He forgives and forgets. It's permanent forgiveness, not temporary memory lapse! Forgiveness breaks down tough, built-up, dirty rotten clogs!

So, by putting forgiveness and bearing into action, you can open up communication once again with your parents.

Dear Lord, communication clogs seem to happen daily at my house. Please help me to hang in there with my parents and to be forgiving toward them so that we can talk about things I'm excited about and things that are troubling me. Amen.

Prime Time This Week

When there are problems between you and your parents, communication gets clogged! But don't let it grow into the ultimate clog: the silent treatment. Ooo. That's no good! Basic communication involves talking! Start with mealtimes, then while watching television, driving to school, church, the grocery store. Just talk! It will get you going and may lead to some new, more honest sharing between you and those people God put you with: PARENTS!

Monday

Do you right now have some garbage clogging the communication between you and your parents? It's time to clear the air! Choose a time when they're relaxed, not super busy or hurried. Open up and tell them your true feelings. Write out what you want to say to your mom, then your dad. _____

_____

_____

_____

Prime Prayer: Ask the Lord to help you be honest with your parents and to give you confidence when you speak to them.

Tuesday

Pray with your parents! Now that you know what you want to discuss with them, plan to close your "un-clogging session" with prayer. Prayer magically melts hurt feelings and draws you closer together. Write out a prayer asking the Lord to give you the words to say and the desire to forgive your parents. _____

_____

_____

_____

Wednesday

Is what you said, what they heard? Or is what they meant to say, what you thought you heard? Confused? Great! That's what happens a lot if we don't make ourselves clear. Misinterpreting what someone said has caused millions of clogs! Try this: Repeat back to your parents what you think you heard to make sure you got it. Now, tell them what you think that means. Are you both on the same wavelength? Give an example of a time you misunderstood something they said and vice versa. _____

_____

_____

_____

Prime Prayer: Ask the Lord to help you understand your parents clearly and not to jump to conclusions before you know the facts.

Thursday

Ephesians 4:31, 32 gives us the do's and don'ts on communication. What are we to avoid? What are we to do? How does being kind, tenderhearted, and forgiving toward your parents improve your relationship with them? _____

_____

_____

_____

Prime Prayer: Pray that you'll be forgiving, kind, and tenderhearted toward your parents so home is a happier place to be.

Friday

Are things super tough at home? Does living with your parents or a stepparent drive you crazy? Read Ken Davis's book *How to Live With Your Parents Without Losing Your Mind.* You can order it at your local bookstore. Hang in there!

Prime Prayer: Thank God today that you *have* parents and ask Him to help you love them as He does.

▓▓▓▓▓▓▓▓▓▓▓▓▓▓▓▓▓▓▓▓▓▓▓▓▓▓▓▓▓▓▓▓▓

THIS WEEK'S MEMORY VERSE: PICK IT! WRITE IT! REMEMBER IT!

_____

_____

_____

_____

_____

▓▓▓▓▓▓▓▓▓▓▓▓▓▓▓▓▓▓▓▓▓▓▓▓▓▓▓▓▓▓▓▓▓

Anchors Aweigh!

This certain hope of being saved is a strong and trustworthy anchor for our souls, connecting us with God himself behind the sacred curtains of heaven.

Hebrews 6:19 TLB

The nautical theme has overwhelmed the fashion scene. Designers are producing outfits in the all-American red, white, and blue. The clothes are smartly decorated with anchors, sailor scenes, steering wheels, life preservers, ropes, ships, shells, anything and everything sea-related. I recently purchased a rhinestone anchor pin for my sister, who works for the cruise line that's "Got the Fun!" to wear to her fancy dinner meetings.

Nautical popularity is particularly due to the cruise ship vacation craze. You can sail to the beautiful Bahamas, Cancun, even Alaska. And there's so much activity aboard the ship twenty-four hours a day! You can swim, dance, jog, go to concerts and shows, and eat. Cruises are known for their breathtaking displays of enormous amounts of food.

Of all the nautical symbols, I love the anchor best. An anchor is a heavy metal device that comes to a point at the bottom making it look like a hook. It is attached to the ship by a strong rope or chain. When the anchor is tossed overboard, it holds the ship in place. The ship will drift slightly with the water's current but can't go any farther than the length of the rope that's attached to the anchor. The anchor holds the ship in place.

The reason I love the anchor is because it reminds me of God. He is the anchor in the Christian's life. We may start to drift away, but a quick, firm tug on the rope reminds us that God is there to hold us in place. God is solid. He is a trustworthy anchor in our life that will keep us ever mindful that we are connected to Him.

> Dear Father, sometimes the wrong things my friends do look fun to me. At first, it seems easy to drift away from You and forget that I'm connected to You. But eventually, I feel the tug of the rope, and I'm reminded that I belong to You. Thank You for keeping me securely in You. Amen.

Prime Time This Week

The knowledge that one day you're going to be with Jesus acts as a trustworthy anchor in your soul. And the Holy Spirit is that rope that connects you to God Himself, tugging on you if you ever start to drift! Well, God Himself can be the anchor in the lives of Christians. His personality and His Word make Him trustworthy! Let's investigate.

Monday

In Psalm 119:61 (TLB) the Psalmist writes that evil men have tried to drag him into sin, but that he won't budge because he is firmly anchored in God's laws (God's Word). How will being "anchored" in the Bible's teachings keep you from sinning and being deceived by an evil person? _____

_____

_____

_____

_____

_____

Prime Prayer: Pray for diligence in your spiritual life so you'll know God's Word, which can save you from doing wrong.

Tuesday

Are you looking for stability in life? Do you need someone you can count on to be unchanging—not moody or wishy-washy? Read Hebrews 13:8 and find out who that person is! What is it about Him that doesn't change? What things can you count on God for?

_____

_____

_____

_____

_____

_____

Prime Prayer: Thank God that He is trustworthy, and that He can be counted on!

Wednesday

Have you ever wondered if God's Word is truly dependable? Find out in Luke 21:33 and Isaiah 55:11. What truths in God's Word do you need Him to accomplish in your life today? _____

_____

_____

_____

Prime Prayer: Ask God to work His Word in your life and to make you open to His will.

Thursday

Rocks are not easily broken; they are strong and they last forever. God is called a rock. Read Isaiah 26:4 and Psalm 19:14. What does this tell you about God's personality? _____

_____

_____

_____

Prime Prayer: Thank God today that He is firm, solid, strong, and everlasting! Praise Him for being the rock in your life.

Friday

God is trustworthy. And because He is trustworthy, you can confidently build your life on Him. He is a firm foundation, a rock. Read Matthew 7:24–27. What are some "sandy," unstable things that people foolishly build their lives upon? _____

_____

_____

_____

Prime Prayer: Pray to get away from the sandy, unstable beliefs of this world and to build your life on the solid teachings of Christ. You can do it!

■■■■■■■■■■■■■■■■■■■■■■■■■■■■■■■■

THIS WEEK'S MEMORY VERSE: PICK IT! WRITE IT! REMEMBER IT!

_____

_____

_____

_____

_____

■■■■■■■■■■■■■■■■■■■■■■■■■■■■■■■■

The Right Combination

I am the way, and the truth, and the life; no one comes to the Father, but through Me.

John 14:6 NAS

■■■■■■■■■■■■■■■■■■■■■■■■■■■■■■■■■

It's only the second day of your sophomore year and you're already late. Nevertheless, you absolutely must stop at your locker before your first class to get your algebra book. You've successfully dodged the other rushing bodies. There it is. Your new locker, number 406. You start to turn the dial on the lock when it happens. BRAIN FADE! You can't remember the combination. Was it 29–15–3 or 3–29–15? Maybe it wasn't 29 at all. You try 15–3–26. No luck. The tardy bell blares in the hallway. Great! You don't have the right combination. You frantically pull on the dial, talk to it sweetly, then threaten to bash it in! Nothing works.

Without the right combination, you can't get into your locker. Likewise, without the right combination, you can't get into heaven either! That's what locks and heaven have in common. You need to know how to get in or you'll be left standing there dumbfounded. It doesn't count to *think* you know how to get in. You have to know for sure.

If I asked you that famous question, "If you died today, would you go to heaven?" how would you answer? Some people would say they've tried to be good, or they gave money to the poor, or they sang in the youth choir, or they visited the nursing home at Christmas. Maybe they think that owning a Bible or going to church will guarantee their entrance to heaven. None of these is the right combination! Why just hope you'll go to heaven when you can know for sure?

The Bible holds the key. It tells us exactly how to get through those pearly gates of heaven. Here it is! Turn the dial a full circle to the left and stop at John 14:6. Jesus says no one can get to the Father, who's in heaven, except through Him. We need to believe in Jesus to get into heaven. We also need to acknowledge our sins and our need for God. We *need* to know we need Him! Now turn the dial to the right, stopping at Romans 10:9, which tells us that if we say Jesus is our Lord and believe in our hearts that God raised Him from the dead, we will be saved. Saved from hell, that is.

Okay, the final turn. Slowly direct the dial back to the left, stopping at Ephesians 1:13. Here we're told that after we believe in Jesus and accept Him as our Savior, our entrance to heaven is sealed by the Holy Spirit who comes to live in us. There it is. The right combination! Try it for yourself right now. Be sure you're going to heaven. Don't wait! You never know when that tardy bell will ring. Believe in Jesus, His death and resurrection, and the Holy Spirit in you. CLICK. The lock falls off, the door swings open, you're in!

Heavenly Father, thank You for making it so clear how to get into Heaven to spend forever with You. I'm so grateful to know the door to heaven will never be closed to me, because I have Jesus in my heart. Help me to share the right combination with my family and friends. Amen.

Prime Time This Week

Jesus is so awesome! He is your key that unlocks heaven's door. He is your SAVIOR! But He's so much more than that. Jesus wants to be your Lord and your friend. He becomes your Lord when you obey His commandments and trust Him with your life. He won't lead you astray. He loves you. He becomes your friend when you open up and let Him in on your life's day-to-day happenings! You develop a personal relationship with Him. You become best friends, buddies, pals. It's a whole new life! So much better than when you were standing on the other side of His door, locked out. This week you'll learn more about salvation and your new friend, Jesus!

Monday

Now you know the right combination to spend eternity in heaven. But, don't get confused! Salvation is a gift, an act of grace and love on God's part. You don't have to *earn* it, but just accept it through faith (it is believing)! Read Ephesians 2:8. Did you have some mixed-up ideas about how to get to heaven? Write them here. _____

_____

_____

_____

_____

Prime Prayer: Thank God for setting you straight and giving you the gift of salvation.

Tuesday

When you have Jesus in your heart, things start to change! Why? Because you've become new on the inside! God's Spirit is in you! Read 2 Corinthians 5:17. What old habits or beliefs in your life do you need to get rid of now that you are in Christ? What new things have happened in your heart since you became a Christian?

_____

_____

_____

_____

_____

Prime Prayer: Ask God to help you shrug off your old self and put on the love and morality of Jesus each day.

Wednesday

Heaven is the eternal home of all Christians. What will it be like? Read Revelation 21. What does verse 4 say there will *not* be in heaven? How do verses 11–23 describe the appearance of the Holy City? _____

_____

_____

_____

_____

Prime Prayer: Thank God today that His heaven will be a beautiful place without tears and pain, just pleasure from being in His presence.

Thursday

What happens to people who don't accept Christ's salvation? They are eternally separated from God, in hell. How does Revelation 21:8 describe it?

_____

_____

_____

_____

Prime Prayer: Ask God to help you share about Jesus with others so they will spend eternity in heaven, too.

Friday

Abraham from the Old Testament was called God's friend. Read Isaiah 41:8 and James 2:23. Why was he God's friend? Because he obeyed and honored God. Read John 15:13–16. Jesus describes how we become His friend. What does He say (verse 14)? How can you become better friends with Jesus? _____

_____

_____

_____

Prime Prayer: Ask Jesus to help you be a better friend to Him by doing what He wants you to do and by spending time in His Word.

■■■■■■■■■■■■■■■■■■■■■■■■■■■■■■■■■

THIS WEEK'S MEMORY VERSE: PICK IT! WRITE IT! REMEMBER IT!

_____

_____

_____

_____

_____

■■■■■■■■■■■■■■■■■■■■■■■■■■■■■■■■■

The Invisible Friend

He is the Holy Spirit, the Spirit who leads into all truth. The world at large cannot receive him, for it isn't looking for him and doesn't recognize him. But you do, for he lives with you now and some day shall be in you.

John 14:17 TLB

■■■■■■■■■■■■■■■■■■■■■■■■■■■■■■■

It's your birthday. Your friends arranged for a surprise party and they pulled it off. You had no idea! There is carrot cake, praline ice cream, colorful streamers, and tons of balloons. At the close of the party, you're all pretty wound up, so you start popping balloons. Some you squeeze, others get sat on, several get traditionally punctured with a pin. Now think back. In all this popping, did you ever see any air come out of those balloons? No? But yet, you're absolutely positive the air did leave the balloons because they're lying flat and shattered in pieces all over the party room floor. Hmm.

What about the wind, which is the same as air, only it's moving. Can you see the wind? No. But can you see evidence of wind? YES! You see dry leaves skipping along the sidewalk, a kite flying high, and traffic signals gently swaying. When a fierce wind kicks up, you see violent storms, the whipping of trees, flying objects! Your trash can or bike might end up in the neighbor's yard! Yet, in all of this, you can't actually see the wind itself. It's invisible.

The same is true of the Holy Spirit. You can't see Him, but He's there. Before Jesus went up to heaven, He said He wouldn't leave the believers all alone, on their own, but He would send a helper, a comforter, a teacher, a friend. And He did. He sent the Holy Spirit. The Holy Spirit used to live with the people, but after Jesus went to heaven, He sent the Holy Spirit to actually live *inside* those who believed in Him. Acts 2 describes the event. It says a sound like a mighty rushing wind came and all the believers were filled with the Holy Spirit.

The same event still happens today. When people ask Jesus to forgive their sins for the first time, and they accept Him into their hearts to be their Lord and Savior, the Holy Spirit comes to live inside them. Have you opened the door of your heart to Jesus? If you have, the Holy Spirit lives in you right now! He is there to help you, encourage you, comfort you, and strengthen you. He is your invisible friend. You won't catch Him walking away or hiding His head when life gets tough. It's His job to be there with you. You may not see Him with your eyes, but you'll certainly feel Him. Like the wind, you'll see the evidence that He's right there!

Oh, Jesus, thank You for sending the Holy Spirit to live inside me. Make me more aware of His presence and His workings in my life. Amen.

Prime Time This Week

It may seem hard to believe that the Holy Spirit actually makes His home in you since you can't *see* Him. Jesus said blessed is the person who hasn't seen Him, but still believes! Now, if someone moved into your house with your family, wouldn't you want to get to know him better? Wouldn't you want to understand who he is and what he's doing hanging around your living room? Of course you would! You have a guest in your house, in your body! The Holy Spirit! Get to know Him, His purpose, His personality. This week's study will get you started.

Monday

John 16:7–13 and Acts 1:8 shed light on the purpose of the Holy Spirit. List His purpose here. Also, stop and think. Have you seen Him fulfill His purpose in your life or the life of a friend? _____

_____

_____

_____

_____

Prime Prayer: Each day ask the Holy Spirit to teach you, guide you, help you, and fill you with His power in all you do.

Tuesday

What kind of personality does the Holy Spirit have? Read the description in Galatians 5:22. Nice guy, huh? In John 14:26 the Holy Spirit is called your helper. Considering the fruits or characteristics He wants to develop in you, how will this help you in your life and in your relationships? (Hint: The fruit of self-control will help you hold your tongue when you're angry, etc.)

_____

_____

_____

_____

Prime Prayer: Which fruit do you need the most today? Patience? Joy? Peace? Ask the Holy Spirit to fill you up with it!

Wednesday

Some kids complain that some of the things teachers teach at school will be worthless later in life. But not this Divine Teacher, the Holy Spirit. What does He teach? Find out what is on His lesson plan in John 16:13–15.

_____

_____

_____

_____

Prime Prayer: Ask the Lord to give you sensitive ears to hear the quiet voice of the Holy Spirit within you.

Thursday

Read Ephesians 4:30. What does grieve mean? What could a person do that would grieve the Holy Spirit? Verses 25–32 will help you. Remember, He is the *Holy* Spirit! _____

_____

_____

_____

Prime Prayer: Ask the Lord to show you if you have been doing things that grieve the Holy Spirit. Then ask for forgiveness and start fresh today!

Friday

Here's an awesome thought. God's Holy Spirit in us reveals to us God's thoughts that He wants us to know. Do both Christians and non-Christians know God's thoughts? Read 1 Corinthians 2:10–16. How does having the mind of Christ help when you have a tough decision to make? _____

_____

_____

_____

Prime Prayer: Let God have all your needs and the tough decisions facing you. Then quietly listen for His thoughts to speak to you through the Holy Spirit.

■■■■■■■■■■■■■■■■■■■■■■■■■■■■■■■■

THIS WEEK'S MEMORY VERSE: PICK IT! WRITE IT! REMEMBER IT!

_____

_____

_____

_____

_____

■■■■■■■■■■■■■■■■■■■■■■■■■■■■■■■■

Guest Author: Lenne Jo Crum

Beauty—It's More Than Skin-Deep!

Charm can be deceptive and beauty doesn't last, but a woman who fears and reverences God shall be greatly praised.

Proverbs 31:30 TLB

■ ■

Life these days is tough. Television and magazine advertisements constantly tell us that in order to be somebody or to be loved, we have to look cute, sexy, model-thin, and be rich! Pretty tough standards. We have become a generation of people hung up with the way we look on the outside but not very concerned about the way we look on the inside.

It's so reassuring to know that God doesn't require a cover-girl appearance. In fact, it's not your looks He's looking at, it's your heart, your inner self. Of course, wanting to look good is not wrong. But just remember, our looks will fade with age, but our inner selves will live forever. See, real beauty is not on the outside. Proverbs 31:30 shares a very important secret. A woman who fears and reverences the Lord is a truly beautiful woman. It's a different kind of beauty, one that gets better each day. This kind of woman will be praised and honored for the type of person she is, not for the designer clothes she wears or the fancy makeup and hairstyle she has.

How do you get this kind of beauty and become a woman who honors and respects the Lord? You get it by studying God's Word and spending time with Him in prayer. This will help you learn about the beauty of the Lord and understand His will for your life. Anything less, no matter how attractive you are on the outside, will cause you to become empty and unattractive on the inside.

Where are you now on the inner beauty scale? Use this as a guideline. Just recently I heard someone ask this question, "If a stranger had followed you the past twenty-four hours without your knowing it, what would he or she have to say about your life?" Did you spread some gossip or keep a secret? Did you go to church youth group or skip it for a party? Did you spend time reading your Bible or get caught up in a romance novel? Did you obey your mom and dad or do your own thing? Did what you said and did honor God? Would that stranger praise your godly example or say you spent too much time on yourself and following after the world? Could you stand to slide up a few notches on the inner beauty scale?

Developing your inner beauty is time well-spent. You are a valuable creation of God, worth investing in! When you make the Lord your top priority, you will truly become beautiful!

Dear Jesus, thank You for accepting and loving me just the way I am on the outside. Help me to develop true beauty on the inside by being a reflection of You. Please cause me to share Your beauty with others so that they, too, will know of Your love. Amen.

Prime Time This Week

No matter how many expensive creams a woman uses and how careful she is with her skin, outer beauty just doesn't last. Why waste so much precious time and money on preserving something that naturally fades? That's just life. God planned it that way. The same story is not so with inner beauty. The time you spend developing your inner qualities is invested in eternity where your spirit will be living forever with the Lord. Your inner beauty will bring glory and honor to Him. Let's get started.

Monday

Read 1 Timothy 4:8. Now, time yourself in the morning as you shower, put on your makeup, and dress for school. How long does it take? Then try to spend as much time getting pretty on the inside by reading God's

Word and spending time with Him in prayer. How do
you think that godliness is profitable to you? _____

_____

_____

_____

Prime Prayer: Pray that you will put as much emphasis
on your inner appearance as you do on your outer.
Then you will truly be a reflection of Jesus!

Tuesday

Check out Genesis 1:31. Each day when God finished
His creations, He looked at His handiwork and said
what? This includes you! Right now list ten good things
about your personality and your life. Count your blessings! _____

_____

_____

_____

Prime Prayer: Ask the Lord to keep you focused on the
good things about yourself and help you to appreciate each of your special qualities while you work on
the areas that need improvement.

Wednesday

The world of advertising tries to make you feel like
you don't measure up! What gimmicks does the media

use to make you think beauty can last and that a youthful appearance can be preserved forever? Are they right or wrong according to 2 Corinthians 4:16?

_____

_____

_____

_____

_____

Prime Prayer: Ask the Lord to make you believe you are a beautiful and valuable person no matter what anyone else says!

Thursday

Look up Matthew 23:27. What do beautiful women with ugly personalities have in common with tombstones? Scary! What are the qualities that make a woman attractive? Read Galatians 5:22, 1 Corinthians 13:4–8, and Philippians 4:6–9. Make a list and work on developing these characteristics in you! _____

_____

_____

_____

_____

Prime Prayer: Ask the Lord to keep you from admiring people for their outward appearance and to look past their face into their heart. Also, ask Him to help you develop the truly beautiful qualities in you.

Friday

As a teen, your friends, social life, and grades may take priority in your life. Read Matthew 6:33 and Mark 12:30. What does God want as your top priority? How can getting your priorities straight make you a more attractive woman? Remember, a woman who loves and honors the Lord is truly beautiful (Proverbs 31:30).

_____

_____

_____

_____

Prime Prayer: Ask God to help you keep Him first in your life so your beauty is a reflection of Him.

■ ■

THIS WEEK'S MEMORY VERSE: PICK IT! WRITE IT! REMEMBER IT!

_____

_____

_____

_____

_____

■ ■

Best Friends

Love forgets mistakes; nagging about them parts the
best of friends.

Proverbs 17:9 TLB

■ ■

Select some lightweight cord in your favorite colors,
then knot it together in the perfect pattern until it's six
or seven inches long. Now give it to someone special.
You have just created and shared a friendship bracelet.
Have you seen friendship bracelets around school?
Have you been given one or given any away to a certain
friend?

I have a special friend, though I've never given her a
bracelet. She lives far away from me, in Chicago, where
she manages a major department store. When she
moved to Chicago she had a tough time adjusting to the
new city and a new job. I heard from her often during
that time. She called me a lot, and I wrote her letters to
keep tabs on her progress and offer a prayer of encouragement.

But when my friend made it through the bumpy
times, I didn't hear from her anymore. I began to feel

used. Our relationship seemed one-sided—my side, not hers!

After months had passed without a word from her, I shrugged it off as if I didn't care, pretending it didn't hurt. Then something terrible happened.

A teenage member of my church lost her best friend in a car accident. They had been soul mates, having shared their deepest secrets and dreams, but now her friend was gone. It made me stop to think how I would feel if my best friend were suddenly taken away forever.

Surely life is too valuable to lose contact with special people or to waste precious time being mad at someone or to treat others fairly only if they are fair to you. Loving your friends means forgetting the mistakes or hurts that have happened. Constant reminding of someone's mistakes destroys friendships.

I changed my attitude toward my Chicago friend and gave her a call. We had a *great* talk! Just like old times. People are what make life worth it. Don't take your friendships too lightly!

Dear Lord, You put friends in our life to have fun with, to share life's ups and downs with, and to love. Teach me to value each of my friends, not to take them for granted, and to forgive and forget mistakes. Amen.

Prime Time This Week

No one can happily exist in this world without friends. A great truth in life is this: To have a friend, you must be a friend. Learn this lesson well. This week you'll discover how to be a friend to others through your words and actions.

Monday

Your words can encourage or discourage friendships. Sarcasm is only funny for a while, then it gets old. People can't put up with put-downs very long. Read Ephesians 4:29. What kind of words should you avoid?

_____

_____

_____

_____

Prime Prayer: Ask the Lord to help you speak only words that encourage others and will build them up to be their best selves!

Tuesday

The qualities of true friendship are the same as those of true love. Read 1 Corinthians 13:4–8 to find the perfect pattern. List the qualities it describes. Work on putting these qualities in your friendships.

_____

_____

_____

_____

Prime Prayer: Ask God to help you put love into action with your friendships.

Wednesday

Girls can be the best of friends or the worst of enemies. Some are experts at being hateful, then loving, all in the same day. Practice being consistent in your friendships. Don't be a Dr. Jekyll and Mr. Hyde. Your friends won't know where they stand with you. How does inconsistency break up friendships? _____

_____

_____

_____

_____

Prime Prayer: Pray for the ability to be the same person all the time, to be your true self.

Thursday

As this week's Scripture in Proverbs 17:9 tells us, love forgets mistakes. Have you been mad at someone? Who? Describe the situation. Are you holding a grudge? Get rid of it now. Ask for forgiveness. Friendship is worth it. _____

_____

_____

_____

_____

Prime Prayer: Ask Jesus to help you forgive and forget so your friendship can grow, not die.

Friday

Do you do special things for your friends to let them know you care for them, or do you take them for granted? Do you want to keep their friendship? Choose three people and list something special you can do for them today to let them know you care. _____

_____

_____

_____

Prime Prayer: Ask the Lord to show you how each of your friends is a special gift and to teach you how to cherish them instead of taking them for granted.

■■■■■■■■■■■■■■■■■■■■■■■■■■■■■■■■■■

THIS WEEK'S MEMORY VERSE: PICK IT! WRITE IT! REMEMBER IT!

_____

_____

_____

_____

_____

■■■■■■■■■■■■■■■■■■■■■■■■■■■■■■■■■■

Total Fitness

Bodily exercise is all right, but spiritual exercise is
much more important and is a tonic for all you do.
1 Timothy 4:8 TLB

■■■■■■■■■■■■■■■■■■■■■■■■■■■■■■■■

"Cathy" is one of the most popular comic strips ever,
especially among girls. Cathy has problems to which
most females can relate. Her clothes never fit her quite
right, her straight hair doesn't curl the way she wants,
her love life constantly teeter-totters, and worst of all,
Cathy struggles with her body. She daydreams of being
a size five with thin thighs! You won't catch Cathy in
"Body Glove" attire!

Cathy reflects the struggles of a female trapped in the
expectations of our current society. Teenage girls especially get caught in this trap. (They think they're too fat,
so they constantly diet; they think they're too soft, so
they try to work out; they think they're not pretty, so
they work to make up for it.)

A balanced diet and regular exercise is good. Eating
sensibly provides your body with the right nutrients to
keep it healthy and feeling good. A good workout keeps

muscles toned, the heart conditioned, and relieves the built-up stress every teen girl has!

The key word here is *balance!* Too many girls get carried away in the diet and exercise charade, causing eating disorders or constant yo-yoing. Have you or a friend declared a dieting war on your body one day, only to forfeit your efforts by the end of the week to a hot fudge brownie sundae? Up and down. Start and stop. It gets exhausting. The outcome is a battered self-image and usually the exact same body you started with. Balance and realistic expectations will be a welcome relief to your system!

This week's Scripture points out that physical exercise is good, but people benefit more when they focus on spiritual exercise. Spiritual exercise acts as a "tonic." A tonic is something that produces a healthy physical or mental condition in a person. It invigorates and refreshes. That's what emphasizing your spiritual development will do! You'll feel better, look better, both physically and mentally, when you focus on your spiritual, Christlike self!

> Dear Lord, help me to be balanced in my physical and spiritual exercise. I know I need to spend more time working out my spiritual muscles so I'll be more like You. Amen.

Prime Time This Week

Teen girls are notorious for being preoccupied with their bodies. There's always something that's not right, in their opinion. Appearance weighs heavily on their heart and mind. Are you one of those girls? Balanced eating and exercise are important. Not just for weight control and figure shaping either! You'll *feel* better mentally and physically with regular exercise. But your spiritual self deserves equal workout time, especially since it profits you more! This week, work on getting these concepts in the right perspective!

Monday

First Timothy 4:8 says a good spiritual life is like a tonic! How? Listen! When your spiritual life is right and in tune with God, other aspects of your life will fall into line as well. You won't be so cranky toward your parents, school won't seem like such a drag, life itself will be better. Put God first, spending time with Him first, each day.

> *Prime Prayer:* Ask the Lord to open your eyes to the true value of your spiritual life.

Tuesday

Your body is not your own! Whose is it then? Find out in 1 Corinthians 6:19, 20. In light of this discovery, how should you be treating your body?

_____

_____

_____

_____

_____

Prime Prayer: Pray that you will be wise to your need for both physical and spiritual exercise since your body is the home of the Holy Spirit and owned by the Lord!

Wednesday

Make exercise *part* of your life, not your *whole* life. Work out fifteen minutes each day, four to six times per week. Consistent exercise has the best results! See my book *Beautifully Created* for more exercise ideas! Go ahead. Start right now! List your favorite type of exercise and the areas of your body you need to tone up.

_____

_____

_____

Prime Prayer: Ask Jesus to give the power to exercise a small amount each day instead of in panicked spurts when you see yourself gain a few pounds!

Thursday

Eat to live, don't live to eat! Millions of females get that twisted around! Feed your body a balanced program, counting calories if you are overweight. No crazy diets, laxatives, or water pills! They never work permanently and usually screw up your body functions! Read 1 Corinthians 9:27. How can you apply this principle to diet and exercise? _____

_____

_____

_____

Prime Prayer: Ask God to help you have control over your eating instead of it's controlling you.

Friday

First Corinthians 3:16, 17 has strong words to say about your body. Read it twice! Who dwells in your body? Does God say your body is holy? How do alcohol, drugs, cigarettes, junk food, and immoral sex destroy your body? How are these things dishonoring the Lord? _____

_____

_____

_____

Prime Prayer: Pray for wisdom to choose to honor the Lord with your body.

■■■■■■■■■■■■■■■■■■■■■■■■■■■■■■

THIS WEEK'S MEMORY VERSE: PICK IT! WRITE IT! REMEMBER IT!

_____

_____

_____

_____

_____

■■■■■■■■■■■■■■■■■■■■■■■■■■■■■■

Guest Author: Barbra Minar

Hope in the Night

For my father and my mother have forsaken me, but
the Lord will take me up.

Psalm 27:10 NAS

■■■■■■■■■■■■■■■■■■■■■■■■■■■■■■■■

Laura lay in her narrow single bed. Her clock illuminated the time in the dark—11:46 P.M. She could still hear her parents' voices. Shouting. Angry. Her mother was crying. Laura put the pillow over her head. *I can't stand it!* Her body felt stiff. She pulled her knees up and curled into a ball.

I'm trying to make everything easier, she thought. *Taking care of Joey every afternoon isn't a picnic. Can't they even try? If they get a divorce what will happen to Joey? What will happen to me?*

Laura broke out in a clammy sweat. *What will happen to me?* Vivid pictures began swirling in her mind. A divorce, a move to another house—maybe another school. Her father leaving. Living with her mother. Spending weekends with her father. Little Joey crying.

Laura turned on the light. It was 1:15 A.M. The house was silent. Laura's tight chest hurt. It felt hard to breathe. *Oh God, what can I do.* Getting out of bed, she searched through the stacks of books on her dresser for her Bible. She found it and climbed back under her blankets. *Please say something to me, God.* She opened the Word and began to read. Psalm 27 (NAS):

> . . . Whom shall I fear?
> The Lord is the defense of my life . . .

Her eyes ran down the page:

> For in the day of trouble
> He will conceal me in
> His tabernacle. . . .

The tightness in her body began to release and she read on:

> For my father and my mother have forsaken me,
> But the Lord will take me up.

Laura closed her Bible, turned off the light and deep in the cocoon of her blankets she drifted off to sleep.

Oh, God, You see and know everything. Thank You that nothing that happens to me escapes Your eyes. You understand my fright and You tell me over and over not to fear. Thank You for Your protection and love. Take my hand, Lord. Amen.

Prime Time This Week

Parents often create numerous situations in teens' lives that make them cry out for the Lord, needing to know He is there with them. This week's Scripture will help you to rest assured that not a divorce, an alcoholic dad, a swinging single mom, fighting matches, a lack of friends, or anything can separate you from the Lord's loving care. For even when you feel that your parents have forsaken you, the Lord will be there to take your hand.

Monday

When Jesus left this earth, He made a promise to all those who believed in Him. Do you believe in Jesus? Then these promises are for you! What did Jesus promise in each of the following verses: Matthew 28:20; John 14:18; Hebrews 13:5, 6? _____

_____

_____

_____

Prime Prayer: Ask the Lord to help you feel His presence right there with you because He promised to always be with you.

Tuesday

Are you currently in a situation where you feel isolated from your family or friends? Do you feel forgotten? Isaiah 49:15, 16 will cheer you up! Close your eyes and picture yourself inscribed, written, carved in the palm of God's hand, *never* to be separated from Him!

Prime Prayer: Pray for the assurance that you *are* in God's palm. Thank God for His love.

Wednesday

Though God is always with His children, it doesn't mean life won't be tough at times. But it does mean that He will be there to strengthen you. Read what happened to Paul in 2 Corinthians 4:8, 9 and 2 Corinthians 11:23–31. None of life's situations destroyed Paul because Jesus was with him. For what tough situation in your life do you need assurance that God's with you?

_____

_____

_____

Prime Prayer: Ask Jesus to be with you as you withstand the trials of life, knowing that there's nothing you and Jesus together can't handle!

Thursday

I know, sometimes you don't *feel* God right there! See John 14:17, 23. Where does it say the Holy Spirit will be? Where does it say Jesus will make His abode or home? Trust that He is in you. Put your faith in Him. He's not like wishy-washy humans with good intentions. You can count on Him! _____

_____

_____

_____

Prime Prayer: Thank God that He sent the Holy Spirit to live in you and be with you forever through thick and thin.

Friday

God also promises not to forsake His children when they follow His plan for their life. Read Joshua's story in Joshua 1:1–9. This is *your* story as well. How does it give you more confidence as you face life's trials? _____

_____

_____

_____

Prime Prayer: Thank God that He promises to be with you—wherever you go, whatever you do—when you are obedient to His plan for your life.

THIS WEEK'S MEMORY VERSE: PICK IT! WRITE IT! REMEMBER IT!

_____

_____

_____

_____

_____

I've Got PMS!

A joyful heart is good medicine, but a broken spirit
dries up the bones.

Proverbs 17:22 NAS

■■■■■■■■■■■■■■■■■■■■■■■■■■■■■■■■

You have PMS? Are you sure? Does it show? Will you
die from it?

PMS, technically known as "Premenstrual Syndrome," is that generally frustrated feeling most females
experience days before they begin to menstruate. Those
crazy hormones get all unbalanced, leaving us topsy-
turvy, like we're on a teeter-totter! Up, then down. High
as the sky, then low as a lizard. Cheerful, then grouchy.
Some females get so bent out of shape with PMS, their
doctor may need to prescribe medication.

Premenstrual Syndrome can lead to another form of
PMS—Pretty Miserable State! This PMS isn't based on
your hormones, but your attitudes. Have you ever no-
ticed that when you're miserable, you feel grumpy or
depressed? Wouldn't it be great if there was some medicine to make this kind of PMS go away?

Well, believe it or not, there is! It's called a joyful

heart! That's exactly what you need to cure PMS. How do I know it will work? The Bible says so. A joyful heart acts like medicine to your body, your emotions, your attitudes, your outlook on life! In fact, many medical experts are witness to the fact that laughter and joy can bring healing to patients' bodies! Science and the Bible agree!

"How do I get a joyful heart?" you ask. Try making yourself laugh! Laughter brings joy to your heart. I asked my teenage friends what makes them laugh: comic strips, old *Saturday Night Live* reruns, joke books, watching their favorite TV show at night ("America's Funniest Home Videos" and "The Simpsons" ranked high), seeing their little sister or brother trying to roller skate or bike for the first time, and certain people—like their grampa or a teacher or a prankster friend. What makes you laugh?

Another simple but effective way to bring joy into your day is to count your blessings. This may sound trite, but it works. Start thanking God for all the special people you know, the special gifts He has given you. Even include the little blessings like a sunny day, new cotton socks, or hearing your favorite song on the radio four times in one afternoon!

Now that you're already starting to feel better, go do something you enjoy. Shop, read, sew, bake, play tennis. Whatever lifts your spirits.

You don't have to let Premenstrual Syndrome or a Pretty Miserable State get you down. A joyful heart is the perfect medicine. In fact, it's just what the Great Physician ordered!

Dear Lord, thank You for loving me whether I'm miserable or merry. And help me remember when PMS tries to get me down, that I can cure it by choosing to give myself a joyful heart. Amen.

Prime Time This Week

Living in a Pretty Miserable State is no fun! Feeling miserable makes you miserable to be around, too! You're no fun to others. Focus on getting out of PMS by discovering this week what God has to say about joy.

Monday

There is absolute and complete joy in Jesus! Look up Luke 2:10. Jesus' birth was good news with *great* joy. Receiving the salvation Jesus offers brings joy. See Psalm 51:12. Plus, the fullness of joy is found in *whose* presence? Read Psalm 16:11. Why do you need Jesus to give you more joy? _____

_____

_____

_____

_____

Prime Prayer: Ask to have the joy of your eternal life with Jesus grow and to help you spend more quality time in God's presence.

Tuesday

Having the joy of the Lord in your heart gives you something you need. What is it? See Nehemiah 8:10.

How does this quality help you make it through each day? _____

_____

_____

_____

Prime Prayer: Thank God for giving you deep-down joy because it gives you strength to keep going!

Wednesday

When the Holy Spirit lives in you, you have joy available to you. One fruit of the Spirit is joy. See Galatians 5:22 and Romans 14:17. How does joy make a difference in people's lives? _____

_____

_____

_____

Prime Prayer: Ask the Holy Spirit to fill you with His joy today!

Thursday

Tough times bring joy! No way? Read James 1:2 and see for yourself. When you don't give up during hard times, you'll be filled with joy (especially when they're over)! You will also develop character and patience. How do you feel when you've made it through a rough situation? How does patience help? _____

_____

_____

_____

Prime Prayer: Ask God to help you see hard times as an opportunity for growth and increased joy!

Friday

True joy comes from doing something that makes another person happy. Who could you cheer up today? Who would enjoy a visit, a phone call, or a plate of home-baked cookies from you? Give to others and bring joy to them and you! Choose two people to cheer up today. Write down your plan. _____

_____

_____

_____

Prime Prayer: Ask God to help you follow through on your plan to cheer up others today.

■■■■■■■■■■■■■■■■■■■■■■■■■■■■■■

THIS WEEK'S MEMORY VERSE: PICK IT! WRITE IT! REMEMBER IT!

_____

_____

_____

_____

_____

■■■■■■■■■■■■■■■■■■■■■■■■■■■■■■

Oh No! It's Sunday Again

Let us not neglect our church meetings, as some people do, but encourage and warn each other, especially now that the day of his coming back again is drawing near.

Hebrews 10:25 TLB

■■■■■■■■■■■■■■■■■■■■■■■■■■■■■■

101 Things to Do During a Dull Sermon is the title of a lighthearted, popular book about church. The guy who wrote it has a sense of humor. I think he must have been one of those teens who was dragged to church or, at least, had some strong parental persuasion.

After much observation, I have decided the average teens don't need this guy's great ideas to deal with their Sunday morning blues. They're doing terrific on their own. They are skilled self-entertainers. Let's see. Marsha and Sue write notes back and forth using the back of the "Visitor Registration Pad." Jeremy draws punklike characters on the back of his bulletin, while Kath writes "I love Mike" in various lettering styles all over hers.

Now Calvin, he's more discreet; at least he appears to be paying attention. The truth is, he's busy counting the wood panels on the wall behind the pastor's head. Occasionally his eyes drop down to watch a choir member scratch his nose. Lara and Lessa take turns trying to kick each other's shoes off under the pew, which of course gives them the giggles and gets them dirty looks from their parents.

What's this church stuff all about anyway? Obviously most teens find church boring, uneventful, and way too long! There's no doubt most pastors are not as entertaining as Arsenio Hall and the hymns are far from the "Top 40 tunes," but there *is* a reason for church. In fact, Hebrews 10:25 urges Christians to attend church and to encourage each other to go.

Why should we gather together? First, we are to learn about the Lord. That's where the pastor's sermon and Sunday school come in. Second, we are to sing praises to the Lord. That's the hymns and Scripture songs. Third, we're to pray for one another. There's strength in numbers!

When we gather together with other Christians, we can be encouraged in our faith. Plus, we are more effective for the Lord when we work together as a group instead of individually.

If church seems meaningless to you, my guess is that you aren't involved enough! Do you go to youth group, Sunday school, help with the little kids, sing in the choir, visit the shut-ins, volunteer as a greeter or usher? Churches always need more help. What do you enjoy? See how you could fit it in with your church experience.

Jesus says we are His body. We are His hands and feet. He depends on us, His church, to carry out the work of the ministry. Step out in faith and lend a helping hand. Church will take on a whole new meaning!

Dear Lord, wake me up to what's really happening at church. Show me how to get involved now that I know You want me to and that You are counting on Your children to help. Amen.

Prime Time This Week

Church is a place where believers gather. They come together to honor and worship their Lord Jesus Christ and their Heavenly Father. It's a family affair! Do you realize that the guy sitting in the row ahead of you is your brother? And the little lady across the aisle is your sister? That's right! Other Christians are your brothers and sisters in the Lord. Get to know them. Don't be a stranger. We're all in this together. This week find out how church can take on more significance!

Monday

Start with your pastor. Pastors are regular people! Call him or her up and make an appointment. Have him explain the significance of each portion of the Sunday Worship Service. Why you do it, and how it began. Have him explain terms you don't understand, like *invocation*, *benediction*, or *creeds*. If you don't ask, you'll never know! Make a list of all the questions you have so you'll be prepared when you meet with him. _____

_____

_____

_____

Prime Prayer: Ask the Lord to give you the courage to call your pastor and to give you a better understanding of the worship service so that you'll truly feel a part of what's happening!

Tuesday

What? You think Sunday is the day to do your own thing? Read Isaiah 58:13, 14. What are the benefits of keeping Sunday reserved for the Lord? _____

_____

_____

_____

Prime Prayer: Ask Jesus to help you to stand firm in keeping Sundays reserved for worshiping Him, even if it means missing a ball game or something.

Wednesday

Read Ephesians 4:11–13. God assigns pastors the job of preparing the saints (that's us) for the work of the ministry and teaching us the things of God so we are mature in our faith! How will skipping Sunday school and church stunt your growth? _____

_____

_____

_____

Prime Prayer: Ask God to help you realize that you need to be taught about Him, so you can grow up spiritually. Therefore, missing Sunday school and church will keep you from growing.

Thursday

Satan doesn't like church. He's always trying to stir up strife. He likes it when people get mad at each other and fight. Now, guess when Satan zeros in on causing tension and arguments in your family? ON THE WAY TO CHURCH! Don't let him win! And, don't fight your parents to stay home. You're going for God! Fighting puts everyone in a rotten, unloving mood right before church. That surely doesn't glorify God! Say to Satan what Jesus says in Matthew 16:23! Write it here. _____

_____

_____

_____

Prime Prayer: Pray that you'll understand you are going to church for the Lord. Tell Satan to get lost and leave your family alone!

Friday

Do you encourage other teens *at* church or encourage them to *go* to church? Or are you one that needs a little encouragement? "I can't believe I'm here." "My dad made me come." "I hate this place." "Let's skip Sunday school and go out for breakfast." These are not encouraging words! Don't let them be yours! Who do you

know who needs some good Christian encouragement?
Why do you think Hebrews 10:25 tells us to encourage
each other? _____

_____

_____

_____

Prime Prayer: Ask God to use you to encourage others
to go to church and to have a good attitude while they
are there. Also, pray to see church with new meaning.

■■■■■■■■■■■■■■■■■■■■■■■■■■■■■■■■

THIS WEEK'S MEMORY VERSE: PICK IT! WRITE IT!
REMEMBER IT!

_____

_____

_____

_____

_____

■■■■■■■■■■■■■■■■■■■■■■■■■■■■■■■■

Guest Author: Karen J. Sandvig

There's Always a Way Out

No temptation has seized you except what is common to man. And God is faithful; he will not let you be tempted beyond what you can bear. But when you are tempted, he will also provide a way out so that you can stand up under it.

1 Corinthians 10:13 NIV

■■■■■■■■■■■■■■■■■■■■■■■■■■■■■■■

"Why, Laura? Why? How could you get involved with drinking, driving, and the police? You—of all people—pulled into this kind of thing!"

Laura hung her head as her mother berated her. She didn't understand it herself. She'd give just about anything not to have taken that first drink at Jeff's party— and the ones that followed. She could hardly believe she had driven the group around town in Jeff's sports car. The police lights and sirens seemed like they were from an unreal nightmare.

But it was all very real. Laura had been picked up and charged with "Driving Under the Influence" of alcohol and a couple of other things related to drinking as a minor.

Tears streamed down Laura's face as she looked at her parents and pleaded, "I don't know why I went along with the crowd—I just fell into it!"

Laura's father spoke evenly, "*You* must understand, Laura, that we know what it's like to be pressured to do something that isn't good for us. You must also understand that nearly every person—teenager and adult—has faced the same kind of temptations. We must each take responsibility for choosing to give in to them or finding a way out for ourselves. It's important that you remember God will always provide an avenue for you to stand strong. He'll also let you pay the consequences when you make the *wrong* choices.

"Paying the consequences this time may help you look harder for a way out the next time you have to decide whether or not to go along with the crowd."

Please, Father, help us to remember that we all face many temptations, and that You are there with us in moments of decision to help us resist making wrong choices.

Prime Time This Week

God promises to open a door of escape when temptation is getting to be more than you can handle. But it's up to you to *want* to escape the situation and to be looking for God's getaway! This week you'll discover who the tempter is and how to overcome the tasties he dangles in front of your face!

Monday

Tear the mask off the tempter! You're on to his charades. James 1:13 says God does not tempt His children. Who does? Read Matthew 4:1–11. In what three ways did Satan try to tempt Jesus? Jesus used God's Word to get "the tempter" off His back. You can, too. The more you know God's Word, the better equipped you'll be to fight off Satan! _____

_____

_____

_____

Prime Prayer: Ask God to give you wisdom to know that when you feel tempted, Satan is working on you. Then pray for God's strength to say no!

Tuesday

Satan is not more powerful than God! And God's Spirit lives in you if you've accepted Jesus. So, you *can* resist Satan. If you resist Satan's temptations, what will he do? See James 4:7, 8. When you resist Satan, what does God do for you? Read 1 Peter 5:8–10. _____

_____

_____

_____

Prime Prayer: Ask for Jesus' strength so you can give yourself fully to God, making Satan run from you!

Wednesday

Satan uses temptation to try to achieve his three goals. Read John 10:10. What are his goals? Satan is out to destroy teens through drugs, alcohol, gangs, evil song lyrics, and suicide. Are you allowing Satan to slip into your private life by tempting you with any of these things? Are you giving in to a few of them? Pray about these things, especially the music you listen to. Don't let Satan trick you. _____

_____
_____
_____

Prime Prayer: If you drink, do some drugs, or have thoughts about suicide, you open yourself up to Satan. You're letting him get his foot in the door. Ask God to heal your hurts so you won't turn to those solutions any longer.

Thursday

Want to see clearly through the devil's schemes? Put Matthew 26:40, 41 and Luke 21:36 into practice! How does prayer keep you strong against temptations? How does it help you make the right choices? _____

_____
_____
_____

Prime Prayer: Pray daily so you will be strong in the Lord, able to resist even the smallest temptation.

Friday

Most temptations start in your thoughts. If you play with those thoughts and carry them out, you'll end up sinning. Stop tempting thoughts immediately! Read 2 Corinthians 10:5. If it's not a Christlike thought, get rid of it. Challenge yourself to tell Satan to scram!

Prime Prayer: Ask Jesus to help you get control over your thoughts, especially those that are evil.

■■■■■■■■■■■■■■■■■■■■■■■■■■■■■■■

THIS WEEK'S MEMORY VERSE: PICK IT! WRITE IT! REMEMBER IT!

_____

_____

_____

_____

_____

■■■■■■■■■■■■■■■■■■■■■■■■■■■■■■■

Hospitality Plus!

When God's children are in need, you be the one to help them out. And get into the habit of inviting guests home for dinner or, if they need lodging, for the night.

Romans 12:13 TLB

Martha Stewart has earned her reputation as "Hospitality Queen" as she has helped the American woman become a better hostess. Miss Stewart has offered elegance to family-style cooking through well-coordinated settings. The Martha Stewart Collection at K mart provides matching dishes, silverware, glasses, place mats, tablecloths, and napkins. Her etiquette and elaborate wedding and entertainment books have kept women at their best.

Of course, I can't ignore the contributions of Miss Manners, Emily Post, or Amy Vanderbilt, who have all taught us how to be organized and proper hostesses. They have certainly done their part to make us feel confident in our party giving and our hospitality.

Christian hospitality goes a step further. It is more

than being a charming entertainer, socialite, fancy chef, or well-coordinated decorator. It's hospitality plus! Plus what?

Christian hospitality is more than impressing your friends with your abilities; it's helping those in need. They may need a meal or a place to sleep. Plus, Christian hospitality extends beyond our regular circle of friends. Hebrews 13:2 says to be hospitable even to strangers—people you don't know very well yet, new friends. Have you heard the saying, "A stranger is a friend you haven't met yet"? Hospitable Christians are always ready to open their door to others, whether they are in the mood or not, whether their house is clean or not!

Sure, inviting your friends over for homemade pizza after youth group or the football game is definitely fellowship we all enjoy. It does count as hospitality. But take it a step further. Be on the lookout for the girl who *needs* a good meal, *needs* a new friend, or *needs* to sleep over to get a break from home. Then make it special for her and yourself. Coordinate your table setting, add fresh flowers, prepare your favorite meal! ENJOY!

Dear Lord, hospitality is not just the world's idea, it is Your idea, too. Please make me willing to open my home, my room, share my things, and share my time with someone who needs it. I want to be a good hostess for You. Amen.

Prime Time This Week

Developing the habit of hospitality is so much fun and so rewarding! You get to give special treatment to others, plus you feel good about sharing in a special way. What attitude does a good hostess have? Are there certain Christians who should be more hospitable than others? What are some fun and inexpensive ways to decorate when you do entertain? These answers and more this week!

Monday

Being hospitable can get tiring because of cleaning up or cooking or having to be pleasant when you don't feel like it. But the Bible tells us how to be hospitable. Read 1 Peter 4:9. How would constant complaining take the joy out of having someone over, for you and your guest?

_____

_____

_____

_____

_____

Prime Prayer: Ask the Lord to help you keep a positive attitude when you are being hospitable to someone else, especially when you know He wants you to help the person.

Tuesday

The Lord wants all Christians to be hospitable. That's why He tells us to be nice to people we don't know—they may be angels! But there is one person God specifically tells to be willing to open his home to others. Find out who in 1 Timothy 3:2. Why is it important for pastors and leaders in the church to be hospitable?

_____

_____

_____

_____

Prime Prayer: Pray for your pastor or priest and ask the Lord to help him or her be kind and hospitable to others, because sometimes it's tough to keep on smiling!

Wednesday

Most young ladies start learning about hospitality when they have tea parties with Barbie and her friends. Yet as they grow up, many females are not very hospitable. Why not? How does it make you feel when someone never invites you over? Is there someone you've been neglecting? Invite him or her over to your house this week! _____

_____

_____

_____

Prime Prayer: Ask the Lord to forgive you if you've been playing favorites with your friends and to help you be equally hospitable to everyone.

Thursday

Extra special touches make entertaining even more fun. And they're so easy! Buy colored napkins at the grocery store that match or blend with a color in your family's plates. Plus, silverware is now available with colored handles! Food adds color, too. Volunteer to help with family meals. Balance the food groups, selecting them in a variety of colors so your meal will look as good as it is going to taste! Plan out a dinner menu incorporating the above ideas. _____

_____

_____

_____

Prime Prayer: Ask the Lord to help you be willing to help with the planning, cooking, serving, and cleaning up for your family meals. It will be fun for you and a great help to your mom!

Friday

Plan a dinner party or a sleep over for your friends. Send out invitations to your regular friends, and this time include two or three new people. Be a Christian with hospitality plus!

Prime Prayer: Ask the Lord to open your eyes to people who need your friendship and your warm smile. Offer your hospitality to them today!

■■■■■■■■■■■■■■■■■■■■■■■■■■■■■■■■

THIS WEEK'S MEMORY VERSE: PICK IT! WRITE IT! REMEMBER IT!

_____

_____

_____

_____

_____

■■■■■■■■■■■■■■■■■■■■■■■■■■■■■■■■

A Spoke in the Wheel of Life

Now here is what I am trying to say: All of you together are the one body of Christ and each of you is a separate and necessary part of it.

1 Corinthians 12:27 TLB

I suppose you've never given much thought to the spokes in your bicycle wheel. I mean, you wouldn't appear normal if you were found sitting cross-legged on the ground, staring at your spokes! Yet, let's be abnormal for a minute to ponder the spoke.

Look closely. The spoke is valuable because it connects the rim of the wheel to its hub. There are many spokes, yet each one is important. If you started to remove the spokes from the wheel, what would eventually happen? Right! The whole wheel would cave in. No more biking for you! It takes more than just two or three spokes to hold up the wheel and make it work. Each individual spoke is needed. When that wheel is spinning, you can't *see* the individual spokes, but they are there working together to hold the wheel up and make the bike move forward.

Have you ever thought of yourself as a spoke? Imagine it. You are a needed and valuable part of God's wheel—the body of Christ, the church. God needs all of us working together with the same goal of sharing Jesus with those around us in order for His kingdom to move forward. As a single spoke, an individual, you can accomplish a certain amount for the Lord. But if you join efforts with other Christians, you can do great things for God. Together, we can keep the wheel turning!

Now, not only are you a spoke in the wheel, you're also a topping on the pizza. Huh? All of the ingredients we put on our pizza add zest, flavor, texture, and fun! Spicy pepperoni, tangy tomatoes, mellow mozzarella, sharp cheddar, bold broccoli, mild mushrooms. Without all the ingredients, pizza would be boring and bland. Each individual topping brings its own unique taste and texture to the pizza.

The same is true of YOU! That's right, you add your unique personality and special abilities and talents to your youth group and your church. Do you bring love, joy, enthusiasm, musical ability, sensitivity, organization, or kindness to the body of believers you are plugged into?

God has planted specific "tastes" in your personality and you are a needed ingredient, an important spoke, in the body of Christ. Your contribution counts!

Dear Lord, teach me to recognize the talents and personality traits You have placed in me to be used for You. Then help me to contribute my gifts to the Body of Christ so we can all work together for You! Amen.

Prime Time This Week

It's always more fun to do things together than alone. That's why God planned the Body of Christ the way He did. Team work. Buddies working side by side. You always get more done that way, too. We're to be "one big happy family" working together (1 Peter 3:8 TLB). This week you'll look at how the Christians make up one team and start to identify which gifts or skills you bring to the team.

Monday

Read 1 Corinthians 12:14–27. Why are there different parts of the body? Are some parts more important than others? What happens when they all work together?

_____

_____

_____

Prime Prayer: Ask Jesus to reveal to you what valuable part you play in the Body of Christ and that you are equally as important as any other part.

Tuesday

Continue today in 1 Corinthians 12, reading verses 28–30. Pick out the gifts listed here. Are any of them your special area? Now read chapter 13:1–3. What is the greatest gift of all? Is it a gift we can all have? _____

_____

_____

_____

Prime Prayer: Ask the Lord to give you a capacity for loving others, especially those who have no one else or seem unlovable.

Wednesday

As Christians, we must all be on the same team since God has only one team! Read Ephesians 4:4–6. List the seven things there are only one of! Now jump down to 4:16. When we all do our part, what is the result? ___

_____

_____

_____

Prime Prayer: Ask God to give you a team spirit attitude so that you will be a help, not a hindrance, to the group you are involved with.

Thursday

We are one body with many functions! See Romans 12:4–8. Identify the seven gifts listed here. Which of these areas do you enjoy the most? Does God use you in that area? It may be your area of contribution! _____

_____

_____

_____

Prime Prayer: Ask the Lord to help you understand that the ability to comfort someone is as much of a gift as the ability to preach a sermon or organize the youth group budget! All of your gifts, no matter how small, are important.

Friday

What projects have you and your church or youth group done together as a team? A work day, a mission trip, a pancake breakfast? What did your project accomplish for the Lord? Now read Romans 15:1–7. As a team, how are you supposed to treat one another?

_____

_____

_____

_____

Prime Prayer: Ask Jesus to help you accept the other kids in your youth group and church so you can truly be a team for Him!

■ ■

THIS WEEK'S MEMORY VERSE: PICK IT! WRITE IT! REMEMBER IT!

_____

_____

_____

_____

_____

■ ■

Stop Checking Up on Me!

Many a man proclaims his own loyalty, but who can find a trustworthy man?

Proverbs 20:6 NAS

■■■■■■■■■■■■■■■■■■■■■■■■■■■■■■■■■■

I hear it all the time. "I hate it when my parents check to see if I'm really at the library or at a friend's. They just don't trust me!"

In case you haven't figured it out yet, trust is not automatic. It's earned. I realize that because you are struggling for independence and privacy, parents seem like untrusting detectives. But before you start shouting "Amen" in agreement, listen to this true story.

Cheri had big plans to go to Mark's party on Saturday night. Everybody who was anybody would be there, even Steve, the cute guy in biology class. Cheri was keeping her plans quiet because she knew her parents wouldn't let her go. She didn't drink much, but her folks wouldn't want her anywhere near this group. They were known party animals. Their reputation preceded them! Still, Cheri wanted to go. Missing the party would put a huge dent in her social life. But, as it goes, the best kept secrets leak out.

Cheri's parents heard about the party through the grapevine. Her mom called around to see if Mark's parents were going to be home Saturday evening. Of course, they weren't. In fact, they were out of town and didn't even know about the party.

Just as she thought, Cheri's parents forbid her to go. She was steamed. All kinds of hateful things ran through her mind about her mom and dad. But on Sunday afternoon, when she heard the scoop about Mark's party, Cheri felt a twinge of gratefulness toward her folks.

The party had been wet and wild, but also wicked and life-wrecking. The noise of drunk kids and the distinct smell of pot came from Mark's house. A neighbor called the police, and most of the kids were in big-time trouble! Arrests were made; parents were called. It was a mess. Worst of all, Cheri heard that Lessa, a friend from choir, had gotten really wasted and a couple of guys took advantage of her. Cheri's heart was broken for Lessa.

Cheri's heart was also glad she had not been at the party. Even though she had spent Saturday evening feeling cheated, on Sunday she was grateful that her parents cared enough not to let her go to Mark's party. Cheri also knew that to regain her parents' trust, she would have to be up front with them, telling the truth about her whereabouts and being wise enough to stay away from questionable situations like Mark's party.

Dear Jesus, I am starting to understand that my parents need and want to trust me. Teach me to remember that the next time they check up on me. Most important, teach me to be trustworthy and to always tell the truth about where I'm going so they won't feel the need to check me out. Thank You. Amen.

Prime Time This Week

Your parents' trust is cut-and-dried. If you lie to them, you lose their trust. If you tell them the truth, you gain their trust. I know teens who purposely lie to their parents. How about you? Do your parents trust you? If so, keep up the good work. Have you lost their valuable trust? Let's look at how to gain it back.

Monday

Proverbs 3:3 (TLB) tells you to never forget to be truthful. It is a virtue to hold tightly and keep deep within your heart. Do you value truth? How do you feel when others are truthful with you? Be honest.

_____

_____

_____

_____

Prime Prayer: Ask God to help you be a truthful person and to be thankful when others are truthful with you.

Tuesday

The fastest way to regain parents' trust is this: Stop lying. Read Colossians 3:9. It plainly states it! What happens when you lie, then have to lie to cover that lie, and on and on? _____

_____

_____

_____

Prime Prayer: Pray that when you feel the need to lie, God will help you through the situation because you chose to be honest instead.

Wednesday

Read John 8:44 to find out who is the originator or father of lies. He will tempt you to lie. Submit yourself to God each day to stay away from the temptation to lie. So, when you're tempted to fib, who is behind it?

_____

_____

_____

Prime Prayer: Pray that you'll recognize Satan trying to encourage you to lie and then that you'll choose not to, because you want to follow God.

Thursday

Read James 3:1–12. What small part of your body can cause big problems? Are there hurtful words you have said to your parents and need to take back? Practice holding your tongue and guarding your words. How will this help in your relationships with others?

_____

_____

_____

Prime Prayer: Ask God to help you be consistent so that there is not evil and good coming out of your mouth, only good.

Friday

Do your friends lie to their parents? Your folks will be quick to pick up on this. Be careful of the influence your friends can have on you. Read 1 Corinthians 15:33. What would happen if you and your friends made a pact to be honest in all situations? (Remember, the *facts* are always your friend.) _____

_____

_____

_____

Prime Prayer: Ask God to help you be a positive influence on your friends, but if it's not working, then ask for the courage to get new friends.

THIS WEEK'S MEMORY VERSE: PICK IT! WRITE IT!
REMEMBER IT!

_____

_____

_____

_____

_____

The Little Brick Schoolhouse

Apply your heart to discipline, and your ears to words of knowledge.

Proverbs 23:12 NAS

■ ■

At the age of nine, Moses Ole Keripei sneaked out of the musty, mud-covered hut his mother built, leaving behind his brothers and sisters, his beloved mother, and his traditional, old-fashioned-minded father. Moses was a shepherd boy who desperately wanted to join in the classes at the little brick schoolhouse in the next village. Because his father wanted him to remain at home to tend the sheep, Moses was forced to run away to be able to go to school.

After several lonely years of selling eggs, then helping a shop owner, Moses had enough money saved to enroll in his long-awaited dream. Now twelve years old, Moses was in first grade. He excelled and was dedicated and grateful for every ounce of knowledge he learned.

Finally, Moses graduated from high school in Narok, Kenya. He was twenty-one years old.

I was overwhelmed by Moses' burning desire to have an education as I listened to him tell his story one starry night in East Africa. As I told them Moses' story the next day, the six teens on our mission team were nearly speechless at the thought of all the sacrifices Moses made just to be in school.

That's not the story in our country. Lots of kids tolerate school, thinking it's just a social place to be with their friends. Many teens create their own day off by cutting classes. They declare a "personal holiday." Worse yet, the dropout rate in the United States is incredibly high. That is hard for someone like Moses to understand. In his country it is a privilege to attend school.

What about God? Does your education matter to Him? Does He care if you go uneducated? Does it matter to Him that some people are indifferent toward school and don't take advantage of their educational opportunities? You bet!

God wants you to learn, to gain information, to become wise. Proverbs 23:12 gives two instructions. First, "apply your heart to discipline." There are two definitions for the word *discipline*. One is "a field of study." It's telling you to put your efforts into a specific field of study—maybe history, zoology, nursing, music. Learn all you can about that field. *Discipline* is also defined as "training or development by instruction." To train or develop, a person has to learn as much as he can, then apply it, working hard to be a success.

The second instruction given is to apply "your ears to words of knowledge." *Knowledge* refers to learning and information. Don't shrug off learning and becoming smart. Be selective about what you listen to. Why waste your time listening to teachings that are downbeat—like trash music or explicit lyrics, or violent movies or horror movies—all of these plant bad vibes in people. Listen to positive music and words with good teaching. School is your main source of learning. Why buck the system? Appreciate the opportunity it presents. Moses would love to be in your shoes!

> Dear Lord, school seems so long and draining at times. But help me to see it as a golden opportunity to gain a valuable education. Help me to be appreciative. Amen.

Prime Time This Week

Homework. Grades. Cliques. Tests. Being called on in class. Giving speeches. Teachers. Detention. Flunking out. The list goes on. School with all of its good and bad, stresses and thrills, will fill thousands of hours of your life! Whether those are upper or downer hours will depend on how you react to it all. Do keep this in mind: The Lord wants you to learn, to become wise, to give it your best effort. This week you'll find out why.

Monday

Do you know that wisdom, understanding, and knowledge will give you discretion? Read Proverbs 5:1, 2.

Discretion is the ability to make wise choices, smart decisions. How will discretion help you in your life? What happens if you refuse to be taught to understand? ___

_____

_____

_____

Prime Prayer: Ask God for a continuing desire to learn so that you'll have discretion.

Tuesday

Gaining wisdom is so valuable! And it doesn't come and go like money or people or possessions. Read Proverbs 3:13–18. Wisdom is more profitable than what? List how wisdom is described in these verses. _____

_____

_____

_____

Prime Prayer: Ask God to help you value your education, to learn to *love* school, and to look forward to college.

Wednesday

Learning God's Word will prove to be more valuable to the average student than many subjects in school like geometry or calculus! Read Psalm 119:105. Does God's Word promise to give you direction and insight? How may this be more applicable to your life than other topics? _____

_____

_____

_____

_____

Prime Prayer: Ask the Lord to help you be tolerant of subjects and assignments at school that seem useless, and to teach you His Word that will truly help you excel in life.

Thursday

Have you personally known any teens who have dropped out of school? Where are they today? Are they working? In trouble with the law? How could their lives be better if they had finished high school? What would you say to try to get a kid back in school?

_____

_____

_____

_____

_____

Prime Prayer: Pray for all the high school dropouts, especially those you know personally.

Friday

The Beach Boys' song "Be True to Your School" has been popular for generations. Take an inventory of *your* school. What are its special features, best teachers, favorite activities? Why do you appreciate your school and want to be true to it? How does a positive school spirit make those hallways and classrooms a better place to be? _____

_____

_____

_____

_____

Prime Prayer: Thank God today for all the things you appreciate about your school. Also, pray for increased school spirit and dedication in the hearts of the students.

THIS WEEK'S MEMORY VERSE: PICK IT! WRITE IT! REMEMBER IT!

_____

_____

_____

_____

_____

Guest Author: Judy Hyndman

Waiting on Dreams

Be anxious for nothing, but in everything by prayer
and supplication with thanksgiving let your requests
be made known to God.

Philippians 4:6 NAS

"Hey, Mom, guess what?" Jenny raced into the
house. "Kathy's parents got her that Arab horse she's
dreamed of forever. Why do good things always happen to other people?"

Jenny, thirteen, slouched into a kitchen chair. She sat
with one elbow slumped on the table, the palm of her
hand pressed hard against her disappointed face. "I'll
never get my palomino."

Her mother unloaded the last of the dishwasher, then
pushed a plate of treats toward Jenny. "Have some pea-
nut butter cookies and tell me everything.

"Now, when did this wonderful-awful thing happen?" Her mom adjusted her chair closer to Jenny and poured them both a glass of lemonade.

"She got it last night. You know how I've always wanted my own horse. I can't believe Kathy got one first. I keep praying, but God doesn't answer. I'm jealous."

"Jenny," her mother said, "I really admire how patient you've been. You know Dad and I can't afford to go buy you a horse. We have to wait for God to provide the way to get one. God knows you're waiting. He hasn't said no. Maybe His answer is 'Not yet.' "

With teary eyes cast down, Jenny played with a cookie, turning it over until it broke in two.

"Jen, admitting your jealousy is a good thing. Now tell the Lord how you feel. Anyway, He already knows. Wonderful things can happen when you lean on the Lord."

Just then the telephone rang. Jenny answered. It was Dr. Franklin, the vet. Jenny covered the receiver. "Mom, you know that palomino mare Dr. Franklin told us about last month? The one you thought was too much horse for me to handle? The owners are still looking for someone to exercise her. Can I just try her out?"

"Hmmm . . . well, why not? Maybe that's the Lord's answer for now, Jenny."

Jenny uncovered the phone, accepting the opportunity with delight. The Lord was answering.

Oh, Father, I know You really know what's best for me. But waiting is hard. Whether it's a new sweater, a dream horse, or my very own car that I want, teach me to wait for Your timing and Your plan. I know I can trust You. Amen.

Prime Time This Week

Why is waiting so hard? Probably because we're the kind of people who want everything right now! Instantly. Waiting isn't comfortable. It makes us feel put out. But how many times have you rushed ahead and done something, and it didn't work out as well as it would have if you had patiently waited? This week discover the importance of waiting on the Lord!

Monday

Isaiah 40:31 is the famous "waiting" passage. What does it teach about the benefits of waiting for the Lord's timing in your life? How is renewed strength an absolute necessity in learning to wait? _____

_____

_____

_____

Prime Prayer: Ask God to renew your weary feelings as you wait upon Him to work in the situations you face.

Tuesday

In Luke 24:49 and Acts 1:4, 5, Jesus instructed the disciples to "wait here." Why? Because God was going to do something special! If we don't wait, how can we mess up God's plans for us? _____

_____

_____

_____

Prime Prayer: Pray that you will be more patient, waiting on God's special plans.

Wednesday

One of the benefits of waiting for the Lord's leading, instead of rushing out to do your own thing, is found in Psalm 37:34 (TLB). How will having honor with God be an asset in your life? _____

_____

_____

_____

Prime Prayer: Ask God to help you wait on His timing so He'll honor you and so that you will honor Him!

Thursday

When we are waiting on God to answer our prayers, should we be uptight, pacing our rooms, worried about others who are getting ahead of us? How should we behave? Find out in Psalm 37:7–9 and Philippians 4:6.

_____

_____

_____

Prime Prayer: Ask God to help you focus on Him, to trust Him, and to know He'll supply your needs.

Friday

God told Abraham He would make him the father of many, with his wife, Sarah. But Abraham's wife continually didn't conceive. So instead of waiting for the Lord's perfect timing, Sarah urged Abraham to conceive a son with her maidservant Hagar. Read Genesis 16:1–4, then 17:15–21. Did God accept Ishmael as Abraham's chosen son? How do you think Abraham and Sarah's impatience affected Hagar and Ishmael? It's always better to wait! _____

_____

_____

_____

Prime Prayer: Pray that you won't jump ahead of God's perfect plan, but wait on God.

■■■■■■■■■■■■■■■■■■■■■■■■■■■■■■■■

THIS WEEK'S MEMORY VERSE: PICK IT! WRITE IT! REMEMBER IT!

_____

_____

_____

_____

_____

■■■■■■■■■■■■■■■■■■■■■■■■■■■■■■■■

Me? A Missionary?

But when the Holy Spirit has come upon you, you will receive power to testify about me with great effect, to the people in Jerusalem, throughout Judea, in Samaria, and to the ends of the earth, about my death and resurrection.

Acts 1:8 TLB

■■■■■■■■■■■■■■■■■■■■■■■■■■■■■■■■■■■■

"Missionary work? Are you kidding? If I'm going to another country, it'll be for a vacation, not for building some foreign people a school or going without a shower for a week."

Alan's response was not an unusual one. Most teens aren't turned on by the idea of missionary work, mostly because it would cramp their style. It makes my heart sad. These kids are missing out. I have accompanied several teen missionary teams to Africa, Mexico, and inner-city missions in New Orleans. I have watched their lives be filled with new meaning as they step out to obey Jesus' command in Mark 16:15, known as the "great commission," urging *all* believers to go to all parts of the world and tell others about Jesus.

"But if I tried to tell someone about Jesus, I think I'd chicken out." Teri expresses the main concern among teens who are willing to say yes to missions. They're afraid they will suddenly get tongue-tied when it comes time to tell someone about their Lord.

Jesus knew this would be a common fear. That's why He assured His disciples that He would send the Holy Spirit to give them power to be His witnesses. The Holy Spirit would give them courage to speak out about how to become Christian and have eternal life in Christ.

Jesus' promise is still good today. The Holy Spirit is always with us when we are representing the Lord. He gently nudges us to speak up, and He miraculously plants the words we need in our head!

Teen missionaries are triple-blessed kids! One, they get the thrill of seeing people turn their lives over to Christ. Two, they personally experience faith-building evidence of the power of the Holy Spirit working in their lives. Three, they get rewarded for being obedient to God's great commission! Teen missionaries are ordinary kids willing to let God use them. How about you?

> Dear Lord, when You tell the believers to go tell others about You, do You also mean me? Lord, make me willing, filling me with the assurance that the Holy Spirit will help me. Amen.

Prime Time This Week

Missionary work is not limited to adults, nor is it limited to foreign countries. The definition of a missionary is simply a person who is serving God with the purpose of evangelism and meeting people's needs. No age limit. No specific location. Take a close look this week at missions. The Lord may be opening a new door for you.

Monday

Missionaries are in the service business. They don't just talk, they act. No lip service, please! God's Word compels us all to *do* not just *say!* Read James 2:15–17. When others see you helping the needy, who do they know you are working for? Check out Matthew 5:13–16. Who could you lend a helping hand to this week? How?

_____

_____

_____

_____

Prime Prayer: Ask God to change your thinking about mission work, making you realize you can do mission work in your local community or school. Then find someone who needs your help!

Tuesday

Read 1 Timothy 4:12. Here Paul has two valuable messages for young Timothy. Yes, young people *can* be missionaries! Plus, Paul explains how to effectively witness with your life-style. What are the five ways to show you are a believer, as told to Timothy? _____

_____

_____

_____

Prime Prayer: Pray that everything you do and say will show you are a Christian who loves God.

Wednesday

How is a missionary's attitude to be like Jesus'? Read Matthew 20:28. Missionaries live to serve! It's an attitude that brings satisfaction. Missionaries benefit through personal growth from the challenges they face, and also from learning about another culture. Plus, missionary work can be just plain fun! How could you have a missionary attitude around your house? How would it improve your relationship with your parents and family members? _____

_____

_____

_____

Prime Prayer: Ask the Lord to give your attitude of service a boost, so you'll be even more willing to help out around the house!

Thursday

Come on now, let's get down to the nitty-gritty. Does God *really* need *you* to be a teen missionary? Read Matthew 9:37, 38. Yes! God needs all of us being obedient, doing our part in fulfilling the great commission in Mark 16:15. Describe how you feel about the idea of being a missionary. _____

_____

_____

_____

Prime Prayer: Ask God to give you the desire to be a teen missionary and to make you more aware of being a missionary right where you are!

Friday

Read Matthew 25:31–40. List the five practical ways God wants you to meet the needs of others. Plus, *who* does Jesus say you are *really* serving when you do helpful things for others? Now read verses 41–46. How does Jesus react to people who never help others who need it? _____

_____

_____

_____

Prime Prayer: Ask God to help you understand that you don't have to go overseas to be a missionary. All you have to do is be obedient to the things He asks you to do in the above verses, which you can do anywhere!

██

THIS WEEK'S MEMORY VERSE: PICK IT! WRITE IT! REMEMBER IT!

_____

_____

_____

_____

_____

██

Sunglasses and Sex

Guide me with your laws so that I will not be overcome by evil.

Psalm 119:133 TLB

■ ■

Petal pink rims with mirrored lenses. Shiny gold rims
with deep green lenses. Basic black rims with smoky
gray lenses. My sunglasses. I adore them. I treat them
like collector's items. I have them in colors that match
my favorite outfits like royal blue, red, pink, black,
white. They are also each a different style so I can use
them to match my mood. If I'm in an outgoing, sporty
mood, the racy red pair are best. If I'm in a quiet, sub-
dued mood, I choose the black pair. My sunglasses also
make great headbands. They are a decorative and fun
way to keep my hair out of my face on windy days.

Even though I enjoy my sunglasses for all of these
reasons, of course, the main reason I wear them is for
protection. Sunglasses protect my eyes from the sun's
harmful ultraviolet rays. They also protect against dust,

dirt, and wind—especially important to me because I wear contact lenses. Everyone's eyes need the protection sunglasses provide.

So, what do sunglasses and sex have in common? Well, God's laws and instructions to us are like sunglasses. They are given to protect us from harm. For instance, when God's Word says to tell the truth, it is to protect us from a snowball of lies that will eventually explode in our faces! Lying can break friendships and break hearts. That's not what God wants for us. He wants to protect us from evil. So He tells us to stop stretching the truth and fight the urge to fib!

Now, did you know that the darker the sunglasses' lenses are, the more protection they provide? The same is true for God's guidelines. The stronger the instruction is, the greater protection it is intended to provide.

Here's an example. God's instruction to be kind to others will protect us from being lonely and friendless. That's very important. But God's stronger instruction to save sex for marriage is given to protect us from much greater pain than being lonely. It protects us from shattering our self-image, developing a bad reputation, getting AIDS or some other sexually transmitted diseases, and it also protects against teen pregnancy. God gives us instruction that will protect us from the heartbreak of these consequences.

You may think God's laws and instructions are stuffy and mean. You may think they are rigid and outdated. But think again. God gives His protective instructions because He loves us so much.

I've heard it from more than one teen. At first, they

think it's great their parents don't have any reins on them. They can come and go as they like, do what they want. But pretty soon they catch on. Their parents just don't care what they do or where they go. Those kids end up feeling unloved. God loves you. And He doesn't want to see you needlessly suffer or hurt, so He gives you rules to follow. He protects because He loves!

Dear Lord, I admit that sometimes I think Your instructions are tough to keep. But now I understand that You give them to protect me because You love me. Thank You for caring. Amen.

Prime Time This Week

There's no doubt that God asks you to do some tough things. It may not be what you're comfortable with. It may cramp your style or cause your peers to tease or ridicule you. But it will please God and bring joy to your life. God never asks you to do anything *He* wouldn't do, and He never asks you to do something without a good reason! Plus, He promises to supply you with what you need to do what He asks. This week take a new look at some of God's laws and the potential harm that can result from not obeying them.

Monday

God's laws hit home with us. In fact, this one hits the home itself! Take a new, fresh, nondefensive look at Ephesians 6:1–3. What conflicts result between you and your parents when you choose not to honor their requests? Obeying God by obeying your folks will protect you and your family from what? _____

_____

_____

_____

Prime Prayer: Ask God to help you do what your parents ask, so your life will go well and be long and less stressed!

Tuesday

All of the Ten Commandments are laws that protect us from potentially evil consequences. Take this one: You shall not murder (Deuteronomy 5:17). What is the legal and emotional harm that results from murder? Now consider this one: You shall not steal (5:19). What harmful attitudes does a person have who thinks stealing is no big deal? _____

_____

_____

_____

Prime Prayer: Ask God to open your eyes to the tiniest ways you may break these commandments.

Wednesday

Jesus had a lot to say in His famous Sermon on the Mount. One thing He told His followers was not to judge other people. We often make prejudgments before we know a person very well, and we are also guilty of judging others as if they were on trial in our minds. What does Matthew 7:1–5 say about judging? What does a nonjudgmental attitude protect you from? _____

_____

_____

_____

Prime Prayer: Ask God to keep you from judging others in harsh and revengeful ways knowing that you will be judged in the same manner.

Thursday

What is the greatest commandment of all the law? That's the same question Jesus was asked by the religious leaders in His day. Find out what He told them in Mark 12:30. What are the four things you are to love God with?

1. _____

2. _____

3. _____

4. _____

What would be the possible results of loving God with only part of these? How could that lead you away from God? How does obeying this command protect you?

Prime Prayer: Ask God to help you love Him wholeheartedly, giving your life for Him with all your strength, keeping your thoughts pure and your soul dedicated to Him.

Friday

First Corinthians 6:19, 20 tells you that your body is the temple or house of the Holy Spirit. He lives in your body once you ask Jesus into your life. Therefore, it commands you to glorify God in your body. How can things like smoking, drinking alcohol, taking drugs, premarital sex, carving on your skin, uncontrolled eating, and similar things be harmful to your body? Why do these things *not* glorify God? _____

_____

_____

_____

Prime Prayer: Ask God to make you take an honest look at how you treat your body, His temple, and to stop doing anything that is harmful to it.

■■■■■■■■■■■■■■■■■■■■■■■■■■■■■■■■■■■■■

THIS WEEK'S MEMORY VERSE: PICK IT! WRITE IT! REMEMBER IT!

_____

_____

_____

_____

_____

■■■■■■■■■■■■■■■■■■■■■■■■■■■■■■■■■■■■

Guest Author: Nell Jean Stephens

What a Mess I Am!

God is not one who likes things to be disorderly and upset. He likes harmony, and he finds it in all the other churches.

1 Corinthians 14:33 TLB

Another crazed morning. Paula couldn't help but question herself. *Why is it that I never seem to have the right thing to wear? I look in my closet and everything I see is either worn-out, last year's style, too tight, or lying in my three-week-old laundry pile. And every morning I rush to dress for school, skipping breakfast to race for the bus. Plus I always either forget part of my homework or spill something on it. What's my problem? I'm a Christian. Aren't things supposed to be easier when you have Jesus in your life?* "Help me, Lord!" Paula pleaded as she pulled on her jeans and a T-shirt and headed off for school.

Paula had heard her pastor talk about God's liking things to be in order in relation to the church service, but what about her life? Did God care if she was unorganized and messy? She thought He probably did, but she needed help. She needed some creative ideas to get herself together!

Paula came home from school having had another chaotic day. She looked just like she felt: disorganized and just barely hanging in there.

As Paula lay on her bed that night doing homework, the Lord answered her morning prayer. He put the idea into her head that before she went to bed each night she should think about what she was going to wear the next day and get it laid out for the morning. Then, she should stack her homework neatly by the front door so she could pick it up on her way out.

Paula was so excited that the Lord really did care about her enough to help her get organized and relieve the stress in her mornings. After telling the story to a friend, Paula added, "I realized my room wouldn't be such a mess if I started hanging up my clothes when I took them off, and they wouldn't be so tight if I'd quit inhaling Mom's chocolate chip cookies every few minutes!"

Paula went to bed that night feeling happy and content. It was so reassuring to know that the Lord was not too busy to care about the details in her life.

Thank You, Lord, for caring about the crazy mess I make of my life and showing me how to straighten it out. I want to be the best I can and make my life count for You. And, Lord, thanks for caring about the little things! Amen.

Prime Time This Week

Clutter and chaos sure don't make you feel very good about yourself. Losing things in your own bedroom or spilling stuff on your homework doesn't help either! Pulling it together does take some planning and effort, but the payoff is great. The new sense of organization you'll feel will also give you a new sense of togetherness—a boost to your self-confidence!

Monday

Start today by reading 1 Corinthians 14:33. What does it tell you about God? Right! He likes peace and order. Confusion is not His style. What confusion could be eliminated from your life? _____

_____

_____

_____

Prime Prayer: Ask God to show you how you could have more peace in your life. Then work on those areas!

Tuesday

It's so easy to get wrapped up in how you look every day. Yet, God thinks there are more important topics of interest. Read Matthew 6:28–33. What are we *not* to worry about? Add hair, makeup, and fingernails to that!

What things *does* this verse tell us are important to focus on? _____

_____

_____

_____

> *Prime Prayer:* Pray that you'll be able to keep your appearance simple so you can devote more time to meaningful activities.

Wednesday

Let's talk scheduling. Schedule your activities by the month, week, then day. Use a calendar or daybook. Brainstorm, making lists of what you need to do. Then prioritize the list so you can start with the urgent things first. Start with today!

Things to Do Today: Order of Importance (1-10):

_____
_____
_____
_____
_____
_____
_____
_____
_____
_____

> *Prime Prayer:* Ask God to jostle your memory as to all the things that you need to accomplish each day. Remember to schedule Him in, too!

Thursday

James 3:16 has a message for you today. What two evils are guaranteed to cause disorder in your life? How does envying others' accomplishments or possessions cause disorder? Selfishly wanting to get ahead of others can bring out the worst in a person. How may it cause confusion and messy relationships? _____

_____

_____

_____

Prime Prayer: Ask Jesus to keep you away from jealousy and selfish ambition and make you grateful for what He's given you.

Friday

Face the facts! Most teenagers have messy rooms! Okay, it's your own space, but organizing it will feel good! Start with making your bed. Now look at your whole room. You may need to add stackable shelves or a bookcase to help out. Also, stack your tapes and magazines. Next, on to your closet! Group dresses, pants, T-shirts, skirts, and so on. Line your shoes up neatly. Now do your dresser drawers. There, don't you feel better?

Prime Prayer: Ask the Lord to get you through your organization ordeal. Don't stop until you're done!

■ ■

THIS WEEK'S MEMORY VERSE: PICK IT! WRITE IT!
REMEMBER IT!

_____

_____

_____

_____

_____

■ ■

New Attitude

It is better to live in the corner of an attic than with a crabby woman in a lovely home.

Proverbs 21:9 TLB

■■■■■■■■■■■■■■■■■■■■■■■■■■■■■■■

Spider webs. Musty, old odor. Squelching heat from the sun beating on the roof. Eating in darkness. That's life in the corner of an attic. Can you imagine how awful that would be? Yet, there's something worse. Get this: Life with a crabby female is worse than life in an attic!

It doesn't matter how beautiful, luxurious, or perfectly decorated the house is, it's a rotten place to be if you have to live with a woman who quarrels, complains, nitpicks, and nags! Strong words, but the Bible makes this same point three times. (Check Proverbs 21:9, 21:19, 25:24.) It all boils down to your outlook on life or your "attitude." Your attitude is your mental position or feeling.

In the recent live concert video, "Make His Praise Glorious," gospel singer Sandi Patti explains that she and her three children practice having a happy attitude around the house. Perhaps life isn't going the way her four-year-old daughter wants it to, but instead of pouting, they put "happy" into practice.

Maybe, without realizing it, Sandi is teaching her kids that attitude is a choice. This is a key lesson to learn, especially as a young woman. Master your attitude now, and it will save you a lot of grief later. A critical, complaining, crabby attitude in a woman makes others (especially guys) want to run away from her.

The choice is yours. Choosing, then practicing a loving, kind, caring, happy attitude will make you a pleasant, easy, and joyful person to live with!

> Dear Jesus, it must hurt Your heart to see me overlook all my blessings and go around with a grumpy attitude. Remind me that my attitude is my choice and a joyful attitude is pleasing to You and looks good on me. Amen.

Prime Time This Week

The old saying "You can attract more flies with honey than you can with vinegar" is true! But you can attract a lot more than just flies! A sweet and kind attitude can attract more friends, jobs, dates, respect, and a better relationship with your parents. What does your attitude taste like? Sweet like honey or sour like vinegar? This week's study will let you know about some attitudes you could live without!

Monday

Contentious is another way to say crabby. A contentious female stirs up strife and conflict. She likes to debate and quarrel with others, especially her mom! She is competitive and power hungry. She is not much fun to be around and loses friends quickly because of her attitude. Are you contentious? Do any of these descriptions fit? How does being contentious cause more conflicts in your relationships with your friends and with your parents? _____

_____

_____

_____

Prime Prayer: Ask the Lord to make you see that being contentious is not pleasing to Him and it just causes more stress in your life. Pray to replace a contentious attitude with a contented attitude. Do a 180-degree turn! Run from contention!

Tuesday

Girls are full of excuses to try to explain away their bad attitudes. Here's a famous one: "I've got my period!" Yes, but you're still in control! You can't always blame crabbiness on your hormones. Yes, they come into play at certain times of the month, but that's it! Read Galatians 5:22, 23. List here the nine qualities the Holy Spirit puts in you. Which one do you need today? _____

_____

_____

Prime Prayer: Ask the Holy Spirit to replace the undesirable attitude that you're struggling with today with His precious attitude.

Wednesday

Here are three attitudes that God detests! They are attitudes that are *not* attractive on females. They make you ugly. Check them out: 1 Peter 5:5, 6 (pride), 1 John 4:20, 21 (hatred), Proverbs 6:16–19 (haughtiness). Why do you think God hates each of these attitudes?

_____

_____

_____

_____

Prime Prayer: Pray that you will become more beautiful on the inside by getting rid of rotten and unattractive attitudes like hatred, pride, and haughtiness. Thank the Lord for His help.

Thursday

"She is such a _itch." You can figure it out! This is a common word used to describe crabby females. Don't ever let that be said about you! And don't say it about anyone else. It's not a good word. Stop for a few moments today and search your heart. Are there some attitudes you need to change? Are your attitudes causing problems at home, school, or with friends? List the attitudes that need an overhaul here. _____

_____

_____

_____

Prime Prayer: Ask God to forgive you of the wrong attitudes you've been having. Are there other people's feelings you've hurt because of your attitudes? Go to them today and ask them to forgive you. Make it right today!

Friday

The more time you spend with Jesus and the more you learn from the Bible, the better your attitudes and outlook on life will be. Read Psalm 27:4. How can you reflect the Lord's beauty in your life? _____

_____

_____

_____

Prime Prayer: Pray that when others look at you they will see the loving and kind reflection of Jesus in you.

■■■■■■■■■■■■■■■■■■■■■■■■■■■■■■■■■■

THIS WEEK'S MEMORY VERSE: PICK IT! WRITE IT! REMEMBER IT!

_____

_____

_____

_____

_____

■■■■■■■■■■■■■■■■■■■■■■■■■■■■■■■■■■

Guest Author: Carolyn Johnson

The Visitation

So encourage each other to build each other up, just
as you are already doing.
                          1 Thessalonians 5:11 TLB

■■■■■■■■■■■■■■■■■■■■■■■■■■■■■■■■■■■■■■

"Mother, you can't be serious!" Fifteen-year-old Kelli
stared at her mother in disbelief. "I'm *not* sharing my
room with an eight-year-old for the entire summer!"

"Honey, it will only be for July and August, and you'll
be away at camp part of that time. It won't be so bad."

"But Mom, Crystal is such a leech. She follows me
around like my shadow or something. I want to be with
my own friends this summer."

"Kelli, I don't think she'll interfere with your plans
much. And the reason she follows you around is because she thinks you're so wonderful. She loves having
you for a big sister."

"Well, she's not my sister, even if she is Greg's
daughter. I didn't ask to have a stepfather. You married
him, I didn't."

Kelli saw the look of pain on her mother's face. *Lord,
forgive me. Why do I say things like that?*

"Sorry, Mom. You know I didn't mean it. I like Greg okay, and Crystal isn't that bad. It's just that everything's so mixed up lately. And Crystal's coming is just one more thing. If she just didn't *cling* so much!"

"Honey, I know it's hard for you with all these changes. But maybe it's hard for Crystal, too. She's like a little lost kitten when she comes here—separated from her mother and still shy with me. You've been a godsend for her."

A godsend? Kelli thought about that word. It meant sent by God. It meant *Kelli* sent by God to help Crystal, to be a big sister, to share her room.

"Okay, Mom. If I'm a 'godsend,' like you say, I guess God will help me through it. Hey, my friend Allison has a little sister. I think I'll call her and see if we can get our little sisters together!"

Lord, thank You for the people in my life who love and comfort me when I need it. Help me to love and comfort others as You would. Amen.

Prime Time This Week

There are times in your life when you need to be comforted or when someone needs *you* to comfort them. Life gets tough. Whether it's dealing with a stepfamily like Kelli, your bothersome brothers and sisters, a teacher at school, a friend's ridicule, or feeling lonely, life can hurt. The comfort of others and comfort of the Lord is so priceless at these times. To comfort someone means to give them strength and hope and to help them feel more confident about the situation they are facing. Comfort just plain makes us feel better. And to comfort someone is simple. An arm around their shoulder, a listening ear, a cheer-up phone call. There are lots of ways to comfort! Let's learn some more this week.

Monday

When you comfort others you can cry with them, laugh with them—doing your best to understand their situation. That's called carrying their burden. Read Galatians 6:2. Jesus wants us to strap a bit of their heavy load on our back! Read 1 Thessalonians 5:14. What are three more ways you can comfort someone? _____

_____

_____

_____

Prime Prayer: Ask God to help you help a friend, to say an encouraging word, to be patient as you offer comfort to your friend today.

Tuesday

Read about comfort in 2 Corinthians 1:1–3. Paul and Timothy refer to God as the God of all comfort. It's true! God is always there, on your side, ready to strengthen you and give you hope. Read Matthew 5:4. Write out a prayer today, letting the Lord know of a situation about which you need to be comforted. Now give it over

to Him and let His loving comfort fill your heart.
Dear Lord, _____

_____

_____

_____

_____

Wednesday

There is a specific reason why God so lovingly reaches
out and comforts us. Yes, so we will feel better, but
there's another reason! Read 2 Corinthians 1:4, 5. Write
the reason here: _____

_____

_____

_____

Prime Prayer: Thank Jesus for comforting you so that
you can now comfort others. Pick one person to comfort today.

Thursday

Can you believe it? Paul and Timothy had so much to
say about comfort. Turn to 2 Corinthians again! This
time read chapter 1:11. What did Paul say the people
did that helped him and Timothy get through some
tough times? How does praying for someone give them
strength and hope? _____

_____

_____

_____

Prime Prayer: Pray today for the people you know who need comfort. Lift them up to the Lord, asking Him to heal their hurt, work out their problems, and to give them hope.

Friday

The term *godsend* can stand for several things. A blessing. A miracle. A surprise. Something that comes unexpectedly as if sent by God because only He may know your need! Has a certain person or happening been a godsend to you? Is there someone who needs you to be a godsend to them? Who? How?

_____

_____

_____

_____

Prime Prayer: Thank the Lord for special people and events that have happened in your life just when you needed them most. Now be a godsend to someone today.

■■■■■■■■■■■■■■■■■■■■■■■■■■■■■■■■■

THIS WEEK'S MEMORY VERSE: PICK IT! WRITE IT! REMEMBER IT!

_____

_____

_____

_____

_____

■■■■■■■■■■■■■■■■■■■■■■■■■■■■■■■■■

Prime Topic: DATING

He's So Fine

Don't be teamed with those who do not love the Lord,
for what do the people of God have in common with
the people of sin? How can light live with darkness?

2 Corinthians 6:14 TLB

■ ■

You wouldn't believe this guy I used to date. He ran
a successful business and owned his own airplane. It
was great. If we wanted to go to dinner at a restaurant
a hundred miles away, no problem. We would just fly
there!

More than I liked this guy's airplane, I liked the gifts
he gave me. They made me feel special. Long-stemmed
red roses, boxes of handmade candies, and a silk blouse
I'll never forget. It was beautifully decorated with spar-
kling beadwork. I enjoyed the romantic way this guy
made me feel. But there was this one small problem. He
wasn't a Christian.

Wouldn't you know, it was just when I was dating
this guy that I first heard this Scripture about not being
joined together or teamed up with an unbeliever. My
initial reaction was to ignore it! *No big deal*, I told myself.

But it was just a month into our relationship when the truth of God's Word slapped me in the face.

I found out—accidentally—that my Mr. Romance was dating other women besides me. I also discovered he had a nasty cocaine habit. Of course, he kept these things hidden from me because I was a "nice girl" and we had fun together.

You see, Romeo didn't share my Christian values. He lived a life and believed in things that were ungodly. I suddenly understood why it is important to date and marry a Christian. What's the harm in just dating a non-Christian you may ask? Let me explain. When you start spending lots of time with someone, you may become romantically and emotionally attached. It's very hard to keep a clear head when your feelings are involved. You may enjoy each other's company, but when it comes to discussing meaningful issues, you won't agree. Your values and viewpoints will be different. You won't have much in common. And breaking up is hard to do!

That's exactly the point of 2 Corinthians 6:14, 15. Christians and non-Christians are different. It's like oil and water. You can put them in the same jar, shake them vigorously, but within seconds they start to separate. No matter how hard or how long you shake, they just don't mix.

So take it from someone who has been there . . . no matter how wonderful the guy is, see if he values Christ and the Christian life-style as much as you!

Dear Lord, it's so easy to get swept into a relationship with a guy who's so gorgeous. But

help me to take a good hard look at who I date—
his values and beliefs—before I get too attached.
Amen.

Prime Time This Week

This dating stuff is tricky business! One day the guy
says, "Hi!" and the next he ignores you. One day
you're tight and madly in love, the next you meet
your cousin's hunk-of-a-friend and you're out of there!
Dating is like a hammock swing. It isn't supersturdy,
it's sort of challenging to get on and off, but when
you're on there and swinging away it's fun. But watch
it—when those limbs that hammock is tied to break—
there you are, flat on your rear end! Love is a crazy
thing. But your teen years are a good time to test the
dating waters. Find out what you do and don't like in
a guy. It helps you prepare for the Big M: Marriage!
Yes, that's *way* down the road! This week you'll take a
closer look at the bumps and potholes you'll face on
that road.

Monday

What qualities do you look for in a guy? Be selective.
Just because he's a *guy* and shows interest doesn't mean
he's the one for you! This week's Scripture is loud and
clear. Make sure he's a Christian (and not just saying
he's one because you want him to!). Read the famous
love chapter in 1 Corinthians 13:4–8. What qualities does

it suggest your Romeo should have? (Notice it says nothing about looks!) _____

_____

_____

_____

Prime Prayer: Ask the Lord to help you keep your heart and eyes open for a guy with scriptural qualities.

Tuesday

Do your parents approve of the guy you like? Remember what Ephesians 6:1, 2 says? Look it up! To honor your mom and dad means to respect their opinion. You may not be able to see straight through your dreamy eyes, but your folks can sense things—they may be better judges of character! What problems does it cause to date a guy your parents don't like? _____

_____

_____

_____

Prime Prayer: Ask God to help you honor your parents, even in your dating life.

Wednesday

Dating can often get too serious too fast. That's why group dating is better than one-on-one. It keeps the conversation light and the hormones in check! If your guy insists on being alone, watch out! Keep sex a part of Health Education class, not a Saturday night event. Design four group dates. What could you do? Where could you go? Now, you'll have ideas handy!

_____

_____

_____

_____

Prime Prayer: Ask God to let you see the value, safety, and fun of group dating. Now, be willing to be the one who suggests group activities!

Thursday

The big breakup. Rejection. Definitely a pothole on the dating path! Read Psalm 34:18. Where is God when your heart's breaking? How can He help you?

_____

_____

_____

Prime Prayer: Ask God to help you forgive and forget. Knowing the right person for you may take years to find.

Friday

Girls and guys are total opposites. He says yes, she says no! It's a big problem in relationships today, yet God *made* us opposites! We're not alike. That's so we'll balance each other. Yet, common interests are important. What interests do you value that you want your guy to share? _____

_____

_____

    Prime Prayer: Ask God to help you see that opposite can be good!

■■■■■■■■■■■■■■■■■■■■■■■■■■■■■■■■

THIS WEEK'S MEMORY VERSE: PICK IT! WRITE IT! REMEMBER IT!

_____

_____

_____

_____

_____

■■■■■■■■■■■■■■■■■■■■■■■■■■■■■■■■

Working Girl

Whatever you do, do your work heartily, as for the
Lord rather than for men.

Colossians 3:23 NAS

■ ■

Tess is the hard-working young woman in the TV
series "Working Girl." Tess is employed in the highly
competitive business world and is fighting her way to
the top. She overdoes it most of the time in order to
show her skills and creative talents, hoping to be rec-
ognized by her boss. Her dream is to move up the cor-
porate ladder, to excel in her field.

Tess takes her job seriously. In ending a phone call at
work, if one of Tess's friends casually remarked, "Don't
work too hard," Tess would react! "What? Don't work
too hard? How do you expect to get a promotion if you
don't give it all you've got?"

Have you ever had someone pass this common
phrase out to you? *Don't work too hard.* We hear it all the
time. And what's the normal response? "Don't worry, I
won't." Have you ever said those very words? This
cliché needs to be kicked out of Christian conversation.

That's right. It is directly opposite of what the Bible tells us to do!

Colossians 3:23 says we are to work heartily. That means to work hard, with all your might, purposing to do a good and complete job. It's not the most popular view of work. Most people just try to hang in there until their shift is finally over. They take lots of breaks, bathroom runs, make phone calls, write letters—just tolerating their job. But God wants us to put our heart and soul into our work, as if we were employed by God Himself! Imagine God as your boss! You would work hard to produce for Him and please Him. Yes, I know God may also treat you fairer than your actual boss, give you the schedule you want, or give you a raise. That's why doing your job for the Lord makes it more worthwhile!

In today's world where both Mom and Dad work or a single parent may have to hold down two jobs to make ends meet, the majority of teens have a job of some sort. And, of course, you'll have a job after graduation. The fact is, you have to work for a living, so encourage yourself and others to do their best and to do it for God!

Dear God, I've never thought of my job as something to do for You. Please help me to work hard and to be an example to my co-workers. Amen.

Prime Time This Week

Working is a fact of life! It's a necessity. If you don't work, you won't have an income and won't be able to feed and clothe yourself. In fact, 2 Thessalonians 3:10

says if you don't work, you don't eat! You may not be using your earnings right now to put food on the family table. Perhaps it's up to you to buy your own clothes, gas for the car, tapes, car insurance, and so on. Perhaps you're working to save money for college. Great! This week you'll find out what else the Scriptures say about work. It may change your whole attitude!

Monday

Let's do lunch! Teens are great talkers but beware of chattin' on the job! Read Proverbs 12:11 and 14:23 (TLB). What does labor (work) lead to? And talking leads to what? _____

_____

_____

_____

Prime Prayer: Ask God to help you work hard so you'll earn your wages rightfully.

Tuesday

Active people are eager to be involved, especially at work! But lazy people are full of what? Read Proverbs 22:13 (TLB). What are common excuses for not going to or liking work? _____

_____

_____

Prime Prayer: Ask God to help you cut the excuses and to be a hard-working, dependable employee.

Wednesday

Boss got his back turned? Break time! Not so, the Bible says. Read Ephesians 6:6, 7 (TLB). What attitude are you to have at work? Who are you really working for? Should you do your job half- or wholeheartedly?

_____

_____

_____

Prime Prayer: Ask the Lord to help you give your job all you've got so you'll be a good example and bring glory to God.

Thursday

The average adult spends thirty to sixty hours per week at work! That's why it is vitally important for you as a teen to select and prepare for the type of job you will enjoy. Select an area you love and in which you are gifted. Your level of personal fulfillment will be higher in a job you love than it will if you dedicate your life to a job just for the sake of a bigger paycheck or higher recognition! Read Proverbs 23:4, 5. What do these verses warn against? Give two examples of how money has wings. Check out James 1:17. What gifts has God given you that could be turned into a career? _____

_____

_____

_____

Prime Prayer: Ask God to begin to show you what gifts He has placed in you and the value of a lifelong job that brings inner fulfillment first, a paycheck second.

Friday

A job is a privilege and a responsibility. Whether it's baby-sitting, a paper route, lawn care, stocking grocery shelves, or flipping burgers, an honest day's work makes you feel good. Just think, you've helped someone out and got paid for it! As Colossians 3:23 reminds, it's not *what* you do, it's how you do it!

_____

_____

_____

_____

Prime Prayer: Pray today for your friends or parents who are struggling with their jobs. Ask God to help them see value in what they do and put joy in their hearts for doing it.

■■■■■■■■■■■■■■■■■■■■■■■■■■■■■■■

THIS WEEK'S MEMORY VERSE: PICK IT! WRITE IT! REMEMBER IT!

_____

_____

_____

_____

_____

■■■■■■■■■■■■■■■■■■■■■■■■■■■■■■■

Playful Pups

Teach a child to choose the right path, and when he
is older he will remain upon it.

Proverbs 22:6 TLB

■ ■

Last summer, Molly, our golden retriever, gave birth
to six adorable little puppies. They were so tiny and
totally helpless, depending on Molly to feed and protect
them.

About three weeks after their grand entrance into the
world, Whitey, Powder Blue, Blackie, Big Red, Pinkie,
and Brownie (we named them by their collar color) no
longer wanted to be confined to the plywood box they
had been living in. They wanted out! They wanted to go
exploring, be independent, especially since the stuff
outside their box looked so appealing.

Well, this is where Bill and I had to step in to help
mommy Molly control her pups! Bill nailed more plywood to the sides of the box making it higher. Still, this
only presented a new challenge to the pups. With de-
termination in their eyes, they'd figure out a way to escape. We'd add more height. To our amazement, they

still figured out how to work their tiny toenails into the wood, pull themselves up, and flip to the floor on the other side.

We weren't trying to spoil the puppies' fun or to make them live our way. We just didn't want them to get into all the rubble surrounding their box because it could hurt them. Plastic to chew, stacked chairs that could fall on them, cord to get tangled up in, or even a button or tack that had fallen on the floor that they could swallow.

Yes, we know the off-limit parts of the room looked like great fun. The pups could see neat places to hide, high stacks to climb, paper to shred. But it was up to us to protect them from the potential harm that was mixed up with the fun-looking sights.

Is this story starting to sound familiar? Think hard. Parents and teens? You got it. Your parents have to look out for you, teach you, train you, provide for you, and protect you. It's a big job! You may find yourself resenting them if you think they are purposely out to control your life and push you around with their power. But give them a break, think it through again.

Some of the things today's teens are doing for fun—drinking, drugs, stealing, sex—will harm them in the long run. Your parents are doing what God has asked them by keeping an eye on you. God commands parents to teach their kids what is right. God doesn't want you to drift in the wrong direction! I know each of the excited new owners of our adventurous little puppies were thankful we had watched over them. In the long run, won't you be thankful your parents cared enough to do the same?

Lord Jesus, it is Your plan to have parents watch over and discipline their kids. Help me to appreciate my parents more than I do, and help me understand they want what's best for me, just as You do. Amen.

Prime Time This Week

Having the responsibility of raising a child is a heavy weight on most parents' shoulders. They want their kids to turn out respectable, responsible, hard-working, successful, and happy! To do that, the Bible says training and discipline are mandatory. Proverbs 3:12 (TLB) tells us that the Lord corrects us because He loves us, just as a father does his own child in order to make him better. Can you believe it? It even says punishment is proof of love! Maybe you've been looking at your parents' discipline incorrectly. This week, concentrate on seeing ol' Mom and Dad through God's eyes.

Monday

Can your parents ruin your life? Only if they *don't* discipline you! Read Proverbs 19:18 (TLB). How has your parents' discipline protected you from a harmful situation? _____

_____

_____

Prime Prayer: Ask God to make you appreciate your parents' rules and regulations as a form of protection for you.

Tuesday

Read Proverbs 20:20. What happens to the teen who curses her parents? First Peter 2:17 (TLB) says that we are to show respect for all persons. Does that include your parents? Respect is a key ingredient in healthy relationships. How could you show more respect to your parents? _____

_____

_____

Prime Prayer: Ask Jesus to show you how to respect your parents more, and to respect them just because they *are* your parents. That is pleasing God!

Wednesday

Read John 17 and observe the parent-child relationship that existed between Jesus and His Heavenly Father. List three noticeable ingredients. (Hint: teamwork is one!) _____

_____

_____

Prime Prayer: Ask God to help you build a deeper, more loving and understanding relationship with your parents and family.

Thursday

How do you treat your parents at home and in public? Your actions tell a lot about the type of person you are. Read Proverbs 19:26. How does it describe kids who mistreat their parents? How do you need to repent and change your ways? _____

_____

_____

Prime Prayer: Pray that you will cherish your mom and dad and treat them well so you will be a praise to them, not a disgrace.

Friday

In our society, both parents and teens lead busy, separate lives. Make an effort this weekend to show an honest interest in your parents' lives, their work, and hobbies. Take at least fifteen minutes out each day to talk with each of them. Write down their reactions and the result. _____

_____

_____

_____

Prime Prayer: Ask Jesus to help you know and love your parents the way He knows and loves His Father.

■■■■■■■■■■■■■■■■■■■■■■■■■■■■■■■■

THIS WEEK'S MEMORY VERSE: PICK IT! WRITE IT! REMEMBER IT!

_____

_____

_____

_____

_____

■■■■■■■■■■■■■■■■■■■■■■■■■■■■■■■■

About the Guest Authors

Lenne Jo Crum — Lenne Jo was America's Junior Miss in 1976. For her talent competition she recited an original poem titled "Let Me." Lenne Jo is interested in creative writing and in teens. She is a Young Life leader and committee member. She is also involved in Bible Study Fellowship and has served as a Sunday school teacher. Lenne Jo has judged many pageants on the local, state, and national levels. She lives in Boise, Idaho, with her husband, Curtis, and two children, Gabriel and Whitney.

Judy Hyndman — Judy is a free-lance writer and a contributing writer for *Still Moments*. Judy is active in her church and her children's school activities.

She enjoys baking, traveling, and photography. Judy lives in Los Olivos, California, with her husband, Ken, her son, Sean, and teenage daughter, Gwyneth.

Carolyn Johnson — Carolyn is the author of *How to Blend a Family*. She has also written for *Virtue, Family Life Today,* and *Home Life* magazines. Carolyn is a free-lance writer. She enjoys traveling around the country visiting her blended family of nine grown children. Carolyn and her husband, Harry, live in Solvang, California.

Barbra Minar — Barbra is the author of *Unrealistic Expectations: Capturing the Thief of a Woman's Joy*. Barbra has also written several children's books and had articles appear in *Today's Christian Woman*. Barbra enjoys artwork and sharing a cup of tea with friends. She is the mother of three grown children. Barbra and her husband, Gary, live in Solvang, California.

Karen J. Sandvig — Karen is the author of *Falling Into the Big L* and *You're What? Help and Hope for Pregnant Teens*. She has also created *Crying Out Loud* and other videos. Karen is the mother of two teenage sons. Karen, her husband, Doug, and the boys, Matt and Luke, live in Santa Ynez, California.

Nell Jean Stephens — Nell has received the Teacher of the Year Award several times for her outstanding work as a fourth grade teacher. Nell is a former Young Life volunteer. She enjoys singing, reading, tutoring, and golden retrievers. She is the mother of two grown children and she is Andrea Stephens's mom-in-law. Nell lives in West Memphis, Arkansas.

Has your study time challenged you and made you think about your life and important issues in a new way? Do you have some tough questions that need answers? Terrific! Asking questions shows you care. If you need help getting those questions answered, please write. My husband and I will do our best to help you out. We look forward to hearing from you!

Reverend Bill and Andrea Stephens
P.O. Box 3080
Covington, LA 70434